Houghton
Mifflin
Harcourt

ENGLISH 3D

LANGUAGE & WRITING
PORTFOLIO

COURSE B • VOLUME 1

Printed in the U.S.A.

ISBN-978-0-545-82306-7

8 9 10 18559 24 23 22 21 20 19

4510005722   C D E F G

TABLE OF CONTENTS

Welcome to *English 3D*

*Take this survey to preview the Issues. After each Issue,
check back to see if your ideas or perspectives have changed.*

1 GAMING

**Check the statements that you think are
effects of playing video games.**

☐ improved coordination

☐ strong problem-solving skills

☐ poor social skills or no friends

☐ violent behavior

2 HEALTHY CHOICES

**What's your favorite school meal? Do you consider it
healthy or junk food?**

My favorite school meal is _____

_____

I consider it (healthy/junk) _____

food because _____

_____

3 STREET ART

**Check the punishment that you think is most
appropriate for someone who paints graffiti
on a building.**

☐ a warning

☐ $500 fine

☐ 2 months in jail

☐ $1,000 fine and 6 months in jail

4 PLASTIC POLLUTION

Which of these materials do you recycle at home or school? Write **R** if you recycle them. Write **T** if you trash them.

_____ soda cans

_____ glass bottles

_____ plastic water bottles

_____ plastic bags

_____ paper

5 TEXTING

Check the ways that you stay in touch with people you care about.

☐ talking in person

☐ talking on the phone

☐ text messaging

☐ sending emails

☐ writing letters

☐ online video chatting

6 FAST FRIENDS

Who is your best friend? Why are you friends?

My best friend is _____

We are friends because _____

_____

_____

Learning & Language Objectives

Here's what you'll learn in English 3D! As you complete each Issue, check your learning against these objectives.

BUILDING CONCEPTS & LANGUAGE

- ☑ Discuss **topics** using academic language and present-tense verbs.
- ☑ Learn the meanings of **unknown words** and use them in complete sentences.
- ☑ Follow rules for taking turns in **academic conversations** and ask others to share ideas.
- ☑ Take notes using **graphic organizers**.
- ☑ Respond to **questions** and state **perspectives** using precise words, nouns, adjectives, present-tense verbs, and verbs with *–ing* endings.
- ☑ Listen closely and take notes on **classmates' ideas**.
- ☑ Write **responses** with a claim and two supporting details.

ANALYZING & DISCUSSING TEXT

- ☑ Read **grade-level texts** closely.
- ☑ View **multimedia** closely.
- ☑ Discuss the **key ideas and details** of texts using academic vocabulary and simple present-tense verbs.
- ☑ Restate **details** from texts using precise synonyms.
- ☑ Analyze **key ideas** and **authors' choices** using text evidence.

ACADEMIC WRITING

- ☑ Analyze **student models** to understand the text structure of various types of writing.

- ☑ Use **transitions** to introduce and connect ideas.

- ☑ Follow rules of **standard English grammar.**

- ☑ Write **arguments** to support claims with clear reasons and relevant evidence.

- ☑ Write **informative texts** to summarize texts and examine topics with relevant information.

- ☑ Write **narratives** to describe experiences or events with descriptive details.

- ☑ Use **scoring guides** to evaluate your own writing and classmates' writing.

- ☑ Revise, edit, and proofread **academic writing.**

PRESENTING IDEAS

- ☑ Write **argument, informative, and narrative speeches** using precise words and academic language.

- ☑ Present speeches using **appropriate eye contact**, **adequate volume**, and **clear pronunciation.**

- ☑ Listen closely to **classmates' speeches** and make sure you understand their ideas.

- ☑ Use **visuals** and **multimedia** to support ideas.

- ☑ Use **scoring guides** to evaluate speeches.

Issue 1 Gaming

LEARNING & LANGUAGE GOALS
Check your learning in this Issue against the objectives on pages 6–7.

CAN **VIDEO GAMES** TAKE YOUR **BRAIN** TO THE NEXT **LEVEL?**

BUILD KNOWLEDGE
Read the overview (*Issues,* p. 4).

BRAINSTORM IDEAS
Write a quick list of ways that people play video games.

- on social networking sites (0) _____
- _____

- _____
- _____

EXCHANGE IDEAS
Use the frames to discuss ideas with your group. Listen attentively and record the strongest ideas to complete the chart.

Language to FACILITATE DISCUSSION

So, _____, what do you think?

_____, what idea did you come up with?

1. Teens play video games (alone/with others) at _____ (**noun:** after-school programs)

2. Teens also play video games (alone/with others) on _____ (**noun**)

3. Some students play video games (alone/with others) on _____ (**noun**)

4. _____ (**Noun**) is another place students play video games (alone/with others).

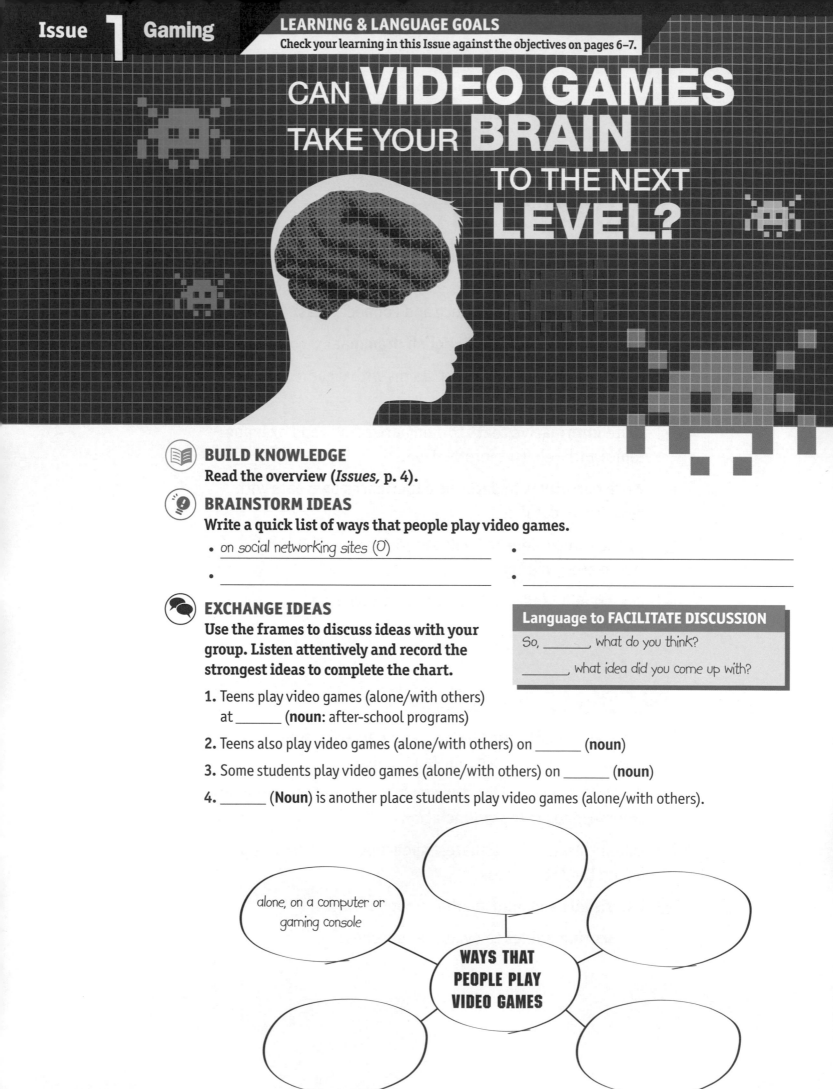

alone, on a computer or gaming console

WAYS THAT PEOPLE PLAY VIDEO GAMES

Words to Know

Language to LISTEN ACTIVELY

What idea did you add?

I added _____.

Language to COMPARE

Our example is similar to _____ and _____'s.

Building Community

1. I work effectively with a partner who is _____ and _____
(adjective: attentive, considerate)   (adjective: organized, curious)

2. I can be an effective lesson partner by _____
(verb + -ing: concentrating, contributing, listening)

3. Learning how to interact and collaborate with others will help me later in life when I work

with _____
(adjective + noun: a demanding manager, an inexperienced coworker, an unfamiliar classmate)

 BUILD WORD KNOWLEDGE

Rate your word knowledge. Then discuss meanings and examples with your partner.

		① Don't Know	② Recognize	③ Familiar	④ Know

Words to Know	Meanings	Examples
1 **interactive** *adjective* ① ② ③ ④	referring to technology that allows people to _____ something or use it to _____ to other people	The **interactive** feature of the museum exhibit allows you to _____ _____ I can _____ _____ because the game is **interactive**.
2 **social** *adjective* ① ② ③ ④	having to do with the way people _____ with _____	People with strong **social** skills usually feel comfortable _____ _____ **Social** people tend to _____ _____
3 **violent** *adjective* ① ② ③ ④	involving actions that are likely to _____ or _____ other people	Because of the **violent** tsunami, thousands of people _____ People who commit **violent** crimes should _____ _____

Language to FACILITATE DISCUSSION

I've never seen or heard the word _____.

I recognize the word _____ but need to learn how to use it.

I can use _____ in a sentence. For example, _____.

I know that the word _____ means _____.

We are unfamiliar with the word _____.

We recognize the word _____, but we would benefit from a review of what it means and how to use it.

We think _____ means _____.

Building Concepts

DEVELOP UNDERSTANDING
Complete the organizer to build your knowledge of the concept.

addiction *(noun)*

Example Sentence

Video games don't deliver **addictive** substances in the same way that cigarettes do, but their effects on players' brains can still create a powerful **addiction.**

Synonyms	Word Family
Everyday: Precise: • _____ • _____ • _____ • _____	• addiction *(noun)* • addictive *(adjective)* • addicted *(adjective)*

Meaning	Essential Characteristics

a strong _____
 	
or _____
 	
to do or have something often
	• doing something even though it
	
	  is _____
	
	• being unable to _____
	
	  doing something

Examples	Non-Examples
• smoking cigarettes but wanting to quit • not having enough money *because of* gambling • _____ _____ _____	• refusing to try cigarettes • buying a lottery ticket once or twice a year • _____ _____ _____

Write About It

When teens develop an **addiction** to video games, the urge to play _____

is more important than _____

and _____

As a result, **addicted** teens sometimes start to _____

and _____

Language to FACILITATE DISCUSSION	**Language to LISTEN ACTIVELY**
I choose _____. I select _____.	What idea did you add? I added _____.

Building Community

1. Making eye contact communicates that I am _____ and
   (adjective: respectful, alert)

   _____ It lets the speaker know that I truly _____ .
   (adjective: focused, attentive)   (present-tense verb: want, respect, am)

   _____

   _____

2. Leaning toward my partner shows that I am _____
   (verb + -ing: listening, giving, paying)

   _____

   _____

   It also makes it easier to _____
   (base verb: hear, speak, understand)

   _____

   _____

BUILD KNOWLEDGE

Read and respond to the Data File (*Issues,* p. 5). Use the frames to discuss ideas with your partner.

1. One finding that caught my attention is _____ because _____.

2. One statistic that didn't surprise me at all is _____ because _____.

BRAINSTORM IDEAS

Write two new ideas you learned about video games from the overview or Data File. Use everyday language.

1. Almost all teens play video games. _____

2. _____

   _____

   _____

REWRITE IDEAS

Choose one idea to rewrite using academic language.

After reviewing the (overview/Data File) _____ I learned that

_____

_____

_____

_____

Academic Discussion

Are video games more harmful or beneficial?

BRAINSTORM IDEAS

Briefly record at least two ideas in each column using everyday English.

Harmful	Beneficial
• make it harder to pay attention	• something fun to do with friends
• take time away from reading or studying	• can make eye-hand coordination better
•	•
•	•

ANALYZE LANGUAGE

Complete the chart with precise words to discuss and write about the topic.

Everyday	Precise
help *(verb)*	encourage, promote,
waste time *(verb)*	divert, procrastinate,
fun *(adjective)*	entertaining, enriching,

MAKE A CLAIM

Rewrite an idea using the frame and precise words. Then prepare to elaborate verbally.

Frame: Based on my experience, video games mostly (harm/benefit) teens because they are _____ (**adjective:** enjoyable, distracting) and _____ (**adjective:** relaxing, violent)

Response: _____

_____

_____

_____

_____

_____

Language to ELABORATE

For example, _____.

I know this because _____.

Language to LISTEN ACTIVELY

What idea did you add?

I added _____.

Building Community

Lowering my voice but speaking with emphasis and pausing enables my lesson partner and group

members to easily hear and _____ my contributions.
(base verb: comprehend, appreciate, respond to)

_____ instead of using a scholarly private voice
(verb + *ing*: Whispering, Looking, Speaking)

may communicate to classmates and coworkers that I am _____
(adjective: insecure, uncomfortable)

EXCHANGE IDEAS

Listen attentively, restate, and record your partner's idea.

Language to RESTATE

So you think that _____.

Yes, that's right.

No, not really. What I meant was _____.

Classmate's Name	Idea

PRESENT IDEAS

Listen attentively and take notes. Then indicate if you agree (+) or disagree (–).

Language to AGREE/DISAGREE

I (agree/don't agree) with _____'s idea.

Classmate's Name	Idea	+/–

Words to Go

 BUILD WORD KNOWLEDGE

Complete the meanings and examples for these high-utility words.

Words to Go	Meanings	Examples
influence in•flu•ence *noun*	the power that someone or something has to _____ others	A student council member might use his or her **influence** to _____ _____ _____ _____ _____
influence in•flu•ence *verb*	to _____ what someone does, says, or believes	Residents **influenced** the mayor to _____ _____ _____ _____ _____

DISCUSS & WRITE EXAMPLES

Discuss your response with a partner. Then complete the sentence in writing.

_____ had a strong **influence** on my decision

to _____

_____

_____

Write your response and read it to a partner. Listen and record a new idea.

I have _____ my friends by recommending that they _____

_____

_____

_____

_____

Classmate's Name	Idea for *Influence*
	• read a book by a specific author •

BUILD WORD KNOWLEDGE

Complete the meanings and examples for these high-utility words.

Words to Go	Meanings	Examples
benefit ben•e•fit *verb*	to _____ or be _____ by something or someone	Teens might **benefit** from starting the school day later because they could _____ _____ _____ _____
beneficial ben•e•fi•cial *adjective*	having a _____ or _____ effect on something	Using a spell-checking tool is **beneficial** to your writing because it _____ _____ _____ _____ _____

DISCUSS & WRITE EXAMPLES

Discuss your response with a partner. Then complete the sentence in writing.

Installing _____

would **benefit** our school because it would _____

_____

_____

_____

Write your response and read it to a partner. Listen and record a new idea.

One _____ change you can make to your morning routine is

to _____

_____

_____

_____

Classmate's Name	Idea for *Benefit/Beneficial*

Close Reading

Language to LISTEN ACTIVELY

What idea did you add?

I added _____.

Building Community

As an effective lesson partner, I am responsible for contributing _____
(adverb: maturely, equally)

and also listening attentively to my classmate's opinions and _____
(noun: recommendations, concerns)

I have already improved my listening skills because I now make sure to _____
(base verb: ask questions, restate ideas)

_____

to show that I am paying careful attention.

 BUILD FLUENCY

Read the text "Game On or Game Over?" (*Issues*, pp. 6–11).

 IDENTIFY KEY IDEAS & DETAILS

Take turns asking and answering questions with a partner. Then write brief notes.

Discussion Frames	Text Notes

Q: What is the **key idea** of this text?
A: The **key idea** of this text is _____.
	• video games have both _____
	  and _____
	  influences on young players

Q: What are the **most important details** in this text?
A: (One/Another) **important detail** in this text is _____.
A: Perhaps the **most important detail** in this text is _____.
	Potential Benefits of Video Games:
	• can improve _____
	  and _____
	• can also improve _____ skills
	  by working as a _____
	  and solving _____
	
	Potential Harmful Effects of Video Games:
	• skipping _____
	  and receiving poor _____
	• lying about _____
	  _____
	  _____
	• violent games can cause an increase
	  in _____
	  and decrease in _____

Building Community

If I finish a task before the teacher calls time, I should make sure to use the time

_____ If my partner and I are discussing something, we can
(adverb: productively, wisely)

_____
(base verb: share, elaborate)

_____

If I complete a writing task, I can _____
(base verb: replace, check)

_____

RESPOND WITH EVIDENCE
Use the frame to analyze the author's word choice.

1. The author says "[parents] grew up in another century." What does this mean? Why does the author include this statement?

   When the author says that "[parents] grew up in another century," he is literally pointing

   out that they grew up in the _____ and today's young people are

   growing up in the _____ Although 1995 is not 100 years before

   2005, the author uses the word *century* to make the point that parents might not

   understand _____

   _____

Use the frame to analyze how the author develops key ideas.

2. The section "Winners or Losers" begins with a quote: *"Video games are ruining my life."*
   How does this quotation help develop a key idea in the text?

   The quotation helps develop the idea that video games are _____

   and _____ It does this by showing how video games affect

   _____

   _____

IDENTIFY PRECISE WORDS
Review Text 1 and your *Portfolio* (pp. 8–17) to identify words for your justification.

Domain-Specific Topic Words	High-Utility Academic Words
• technology	• function
•	•
•	•
•	•
•	•
•	•

Academic Discussion

Should schools use video games?

BRAINSTORM IDEAS

Briefly record at least two ideas in each column using everyday English.

Agree	Disagree
• can improve vision	• risk of addiction
• some involve physical activity for PE	• other software is more important
•	•
•	•

ANALYZE LANGUAGE

Complete the chart with precise words to discuss and write about the topic.

Everyday	Precise
better *(adjective)*	enhanced, refined,
fighting *(noun)*	brutality, hostility,
ability *(noun)*	talent, aptitude,

MAKE A CLAIM

Rewrite an idea using the frame and precise words.
Then prepare to elaborate verbally.

Language to ELABORATE

For example, _____.

I know this because _____.

Frame: I believe that schools (should/should not) use video games because the games lead to _____ (**noun phrase:** serious addictions, aggressive behavior, more creativity, better social skills)

Response: _____

_____

_____

_____

_____

_____

Building Community

During group discussions, it is _____ that I contribute using a scholarly
(adjective: essential, crucial)

public voice instead of using a _____ communication style. Sitting up straight,
(adjective: casual, informal)

projecting my voice, and _____
(verb + -ing: comprehending, appreciating, responding to)

_____ regularly will help ensure that my teacher, classmates,

and colleagues can easily follow my _____
(noun: contributions, suggestions)

 ## EXCHANGE IDEAS

Listen attentively, restate, and record your partner's idea.

Classmate's Name	Idea

PRESENT IDEAS

**Listen attentively and take notes. Then write if
you agree (+) or disagree (–).**

Classmate's Name	Idea	+/–

Words to Go

BUILD WORD KNOWLEDGE

Complete the meanings and examples for these high-utility academic words.

Words to Go	Meanings	Examples
creative cre•a•tive *adjective*	involving the use of _____	_____
	to create something _____	might be a promising job for someone who is very **creative**.
creativity cre•a•tiv•i•ty *noun*	the ability to use _____	_____
	to think of _____	has given me confidence in my **creativity**.

DISCUSS & WRITE EXAMPLES

Discuss your response with a partner. Then complete the sentence in writing.

My friend _____ is **creative** because (he/she) _____

is often able to _____

Write your response and read it aloud to a partner. Listen and record a new idea.

When I want to boost my _____ I sometimes try _____

_____

BUILD WORD KNOWLEDGE

Complete the meaning and examples for this high-utility academic word.

Word to Go	Meaning	Examples
issue is•sue *noun*	a _____ or problem	The student council debated the **issue** of _____
		In my opinion, **issues** concerning _____ _____ should be discussed more often in our community.

DISCUSS & WRITE EXAMPLES

Discuss your response with a partner. Then complete the sentence in writing.

An **issue** that affects teens who want to go to college is _____

_____

Write your response and read it aloud to a partner. Listen and record a new idea.

Of all the _____ raised by technology, I worry most about _____

Classmate's Name	Idea for *Creative/Creativity*	Idea for *Issue*

Close Reading

BUILD FLUENCY
Read the text "New Study Links Video Gaming to Creativity" (*Issues,* pp. 12–13).

IDENTIFY KEY IDEAS & DETAILS
Take turns asking and answering questions with a partner. Then write brief notes.

Discussion Frames	Text Notes
Q: What is the **key idea** of this text? **A:** The **key idea** of this text is _____.	• playing video games may lead to _____
Q: What are the **most important details** in this text? **A:** (One/Another) **important detail** in this text is _____. **A:** Perhaps the **most important detail** in this text is _____.	• researchers at _____ found that playing video games makes 12-year-olds more • measured creativity by having students _____ and _____ • however, can't say if _____ would make children even more creative

RESPOND WITH EVIDENCE
Use the frame and evidence from the text to construct a formal written response.

1. Based on the text, what conclusion can you draw about the study on video gaming and creativity?

Based on the text, I can draw the conclusion that the study on video gaming and

creativity is _____

The author _____ that the research does not measure _____

_____

_____

Use the frame to analyze the author's point of view.

2. What is the effect of shifting from third person to first person in the final paragraph?

The author uses first person when she writes, _____

_____

Shifting from third person to first person makes the article more _____

and it makes the reader _____

IDENTIFY PRECISE WORDS
Review Text 2 and your *Portfolio* (pp. 18–21) to identify words for your justification.

Topic Words	High-Utility Words
• validating • •	• findings • •

Student Writing Model

Academic Writing Type

A **justification** states a claim and supports it with logical reasons and relevant evidence.

A. The **topic sentence** clearly states the writer's claim about the issue.

B. Detail sentences support the claim with reasons and evidence from texts and the writer's experiences.

C. The **concluding sentence** restates the writer's claim about the issue.

D. Transition words or phrases introduce evidence and connect ideas.

(!) ANALYZE TEXT STRUCTURE

Read this student model to analyze the elements of a justification.

A

B

C

> After exploring the topic of how video games influence young people, I believe that gaming can negatively affect teens' lives. Evidence shows that playing video games damages teens' ability to focus on more important activities such as their schoolwork. For example, the article "Game On or Game Over?" points out that teens who regularly play video games tend to develop serious problems because they are often trying to battle addiction, as about 8.5 percent of gamers do. This is important to consider because one of my friends plays her favorite video game from the moment she gets home from school until she goes to bed. Another potential harmful effect of video games is the way this technology promotes aggressive and dangerous behavior. In fact, the author Oscar Gomez emphasizes that teens who play M-rated games fight other people and harm property more frequently. For these reasons, I support the position that video games are generally not beneficial to teens.

MARK & DISCUSS ELEMENTS

Mark the justification elements and use the frames to discuss them with your partner.

1. **Double underline the writer's claim within the topic sentence.**
   The writer's claim is _____.

2. **Draw a box around three transition words or phrases.**
   One transition (word/phrase) is _____. Another transition (word/phrase) is _____.

3. **Underline and label two reasons that support the writer's claim with the letter *R*.**
   One reason that supports the writer's claim is _____.

4. **Underline and label two pieces of evidence that support the writer's claim with the letter *E*.** *One piece of evidence that supports the writer's claim is _____.*

5. **Star four precise topic words and check four high-utility academic words.**
   An example of a (precise topic word/high-utility academic word) is _____.

Singular Present-Tense Verbs

Guidelines for Using Present-Tense Verbs

Writers use **simple present-tense verbs** in justifications to state claims, provide reasons, and cite evidence. Whenever you use the first-person subject *I*, use a first-person singular verb. Whenever you use a third-person singular noun *(author, writer, evidence)* or pronoun *(he* or *she)*, use a third-person singular verb ending in *–s* or *–es*.

Topic Sentence: State your claim with a first-person singular verb.

 I maintain . . . *I disagree . . .* *I believe . . .* *I feel . . .*

Reason/Evidence: Use first- and third-person present-tense verbs to introduce reasons and evidence.

 Evidence shows . . . *The author emphasizes . . .* *She describes . . .* *I know . . .*

Concluding Sentence: Restate your claim. Remember to follow forms of the verb *to be* with an adjective.

 I conclude . . . *I restate . . .* *I contend . . .* *I am certain . . .*

 IDENTIFY PRESENT-TENSE VERBS

Read the justification. Circle the first-person, present-tense verbs. Draw a box around the third-person, present-tense verbs.

After exploring the topic of how video games influence young people, I believe that gaming can positively affect teens' health. Evidence shows that playing video games can combine technology and fitness. For example, I play a dancing game frequently, and after a few games I feel like I just ran a mile. Another potential beneficial effect of video games is the way this technology can sharpen people's vision. In fact, an online news article emphasizes that people who are nearsighted or farsighted may be able to improve their eyesight while having fun. For these reasons, I reject the position that video games are an unhealthy form of entertainment.

 WRITE PRESENT-TENSE VERBS

Use a first- or third-person, present-tense verb to complete each sentence.

1. I _____ that video games can be beneficial, rather than harmful.

2. A recent study _____ that video games may slow the mental decay that happens as we age.

3. The evidence _____ that video games can also help people with dyslexia read faster and more accurately.

4. When I play video games, I _____ more alert afterward.

5. For these reasons, I _____ that video games are good for our health.

Paraphrasing Text

Guidelines for Paraphrasing Text

Paraphrase a sentence from a source text by keeping important topic words and replacing key words and phrases with synonyms.

Source Text	Key Words & Phrases → Synonyms		Paraphrasing
"She says these findings should encourage game designers to investigate which parts of gaming are more responsible for making kids more creative" (Moore 12).	she	→ the researcher	The researcher says the results of the study should prompt game designers to examine which game factors influence increased creativity.
	these findings	→ the results of the study	
	encourage	→ prompt	
	investigate	→ examine	
	parts of gaming	→ game factors	
	are responsible for making kids more creative	influence increased creativity	

IDENTIFY PRECISE SYNONYMS
Read these statements and replace the words in parentheses with synonyms.

1. Gamers (show) _____ more creativity than non-gamers.

2. The (results of the study) _____ could

(lead to) _____ educational video games that feel like

pure entertainment.

3. However, the study (measures) _____ only one type of creativity.

PARAPHRASE IDEAS
Paraphrase the three statements above using primarily your own words.

1. Moore points out that _____

_____

_____

_____

2. According to "New Study Links Video Gaming to Creativity," _____

_____

_____

_____

3. The author also explains that _____

_____

_____

_____

Organize a Justification

Prompt	Are video games harmful or beneficial? Write a justification that states and supports your claim.

Transitions to Introduce Evidence	Examples
Evidence shows _____. For example, _____. In fact, _____. _____ also _____. Additionally, _____.	**Evidence shows** that playing video games enhances teens' abilities to solve complex problems. **In fact,** Moore presents a study that found 12-year-old gamers were more creative. The article **also** questions whether other activities could inspire more creativity than video games.

IDENTIFY TRANSITIONS

Review the transitions that writers use to introduce evidence. Then complete each sentence below with an appropriate transition.

1. _____ that almost all teens play video games.

2. _____ almost as many girls play video games as boys.

3. _____ about 10 percent of video game players suffer addictions.

PLAN REASONS & EVIDENCE

Describe your claim about whether video games are harmful or beneficial.

My claim: I think that video games are (harmful/beneficial) _____

because _____

_____

Use academic language to restate your claim and write a topic sentence.

Topic Sentence: After exploring the issue of how video games influence young people,

I believe that _____

_____

List two reasons that support your claim and give evidence for each reason. You can draw from the text, your experience, or a classmate's experience.

Reason 1: _____

_____

Evidence: _____

_____

_____

Reason 2: _____

_____

Evidence: _____

_____

_____

Write a Justification

Prompt	Are video games harmful or beneficial? Write a justification that states and supports your claim.

WRITE A PARAGRAPH

Use the frame to write your topic sentence, detail sentences, and concluding sentence.

A

After exploring the _____ of how video games influence
(noun: issue, topic, subject)

young people, I believe that gaming (can/cannot) _____

_____ affect teens' lives. Evidence shows that playing
(adverb: positively, negatively, significantly)

video games _____ teens' ability to _____
(present-tense verb: improves, weakens)   (base verb: create, focus, interact)

_____
(evidence from text)

_____

_____

B

For example, the article _____
(title)

points out that teens who regularly play video games tend to develop

_____ _____ because they are
(adjective: improved, serious, weaker)   (noun: coordination, creativity, relationships)

often trying to _____
(evidence from text)

_____

_____

This is important to consider because _____
(evidence from text or your experience)

_____

_____

Another potential (beneficial/harmful) _____ effect of video

games is the way this technology _____ _____
(present-tense verb: allows, improves, distracts)   (evidence from text)

_____

In fact, the author _____ emphasizes
(author's full name)

that _____
(evidence from text)

_____

_____

C

For these reasons, I _____ the position that _____
(present-tense verb: maintain, support, reject)   (restate your claim)

_____

_____

_____

Rate Your Justification

ASSESS YOUR DRAFT
Mark the elements in your justification.

1. Double underline the claim in your topic sentence.

2. Draw a box around three transition words or phrases.

3. Underline and label two reasons that support your claim with *R*.

4. Underline and label two pieces of evidence that support your claim with *E*.

5. Star four precise topic words and check four high-utility academic words.

Scoring Guide
① Insufficient
② Developing
③ Sufficient
④ Exemplary

Rate your justification. Then have a partner rate it.

1. Does the topic sentence clearly state your claim?	Self	① ② ③ ④
	Partner	① ② ③ ④
2. Did you include strong reasons and evidence to support your claim?	Self	① ② ③ ④
	Partner	① ② ③ ④
3. Did you use transitions to introduce evidence and connect ideas?	Self	① ② ③ ④
	Partner	① ② ③ ④
4. Did you include precise topic words and high-utility academic words?	Self	① ② ③ ④
	Partner	① ② ③ ④
5. Does the concluding sentence restate your claim using new wording?	Self	① ② ③ ④
	Partner	① ② ③ ④

REFLECT & REVISE
Record specific priorities and suggestions to help you and your partner revise.

(Partner) Positive Feedback: I appreciate how you (used/included/explained) _____

_____

(Partner) Suggestion: As you revise your justification, focus on (including/improving/explaining) _____

(Self) Priority 1: My justification needs to (include/develop/explain) _____

_____

(Self) Priority 2: I plan to improve my justification by (adding/revising/checking) _____

_____

CHECK & EDIT
Use this checklist to proofread and edit your justification.

☐ Did you capitalize text titles and proper nouns?

☐ Each time you use *I*, is it followed by a present-tense singular verb?

☐ Did you match third-person singular subjects such as *he, she,* or *evidence* with present-tense singular verbs that end in *–s* or *–es*?

☐ Is each sentence complete?

☐ Are all words spelled correctly?

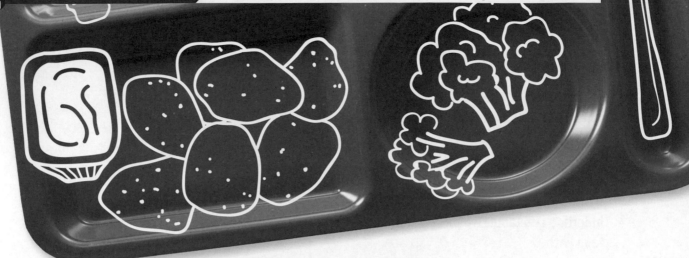

Does school food make the grade?

 BUILD KNOWLEDGE
Read the overview (*Issues,* p. 14).

BRAINSTORM IDEAS
Write a quick list of foods that students eat regularly.

- fresh fruits (H) _____
- _____

- _____
- _____

 EXCHANGE IDEAS
Use the frames to discuss ideas with your group. Listen attentively and record the strongest ideas to complete the chart.

Language to FACILITATE DISCUSSION

So, _____, what do you think?

_____, what idea did you come up with?

1. One example of a (healthy/junk) food that students eat is _____ (**noun:** candy)

2. Another example of (healthy/junk) food that students eat is _____ (**noun**)

3. Some students eat (healthy/unhealthy) food such as _____ (**noun**)

4. _____ (**Noun**) is an example of (healthy/unhealthy) food that students eat.

HEALTHY FOOD	JUNK FOOD
• fresh fruits	• french fries
•	•
•	•
•	•
•	•
•	•
	•

Words to Know

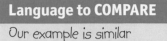

Language to COMPARE

Our example is similar to _____'s group's.

BUILD WORD KNOWLEDGE

Rate your word knowledge. Then discuss word meanings and examples with your group.

	① Don't Know	② Recognize	③ Familiar	④ Know
Words to Know	**Meanings**	**Examples**		
1 calorie *noun* ①②③④	a unit of _____ produced by _____	It is important to eat enough **calories** to _____ _____ If you want to lose weight, you can _____ _____ **calories**.		
2 expensive *adjective* ①②③④	costing _____ _____	My parents said I need to _____ _____ to help pay for my **expensive** _____ _____ The _____ that I want is too **expensive** so I will _____ _____ _____		
3 habit *noun* ①②③④	something a person does _____, usually without thinking	My brother's extreme spending **habit** has caused him to _____ _____ When I get home, I have a **habit** of _____ _____ _____		
4 obesity *noun* ①②③④	the condition of being so _____ that it is _____	_____ who suffer from **obesity** are more likely to _____ One way to avoid **obesity** is to _____ _____		

Language to FACILITATE DISCUSSION

I've never seen or heard the word _____.

I recognize the word _____ but need to learn how to use it.

I can use _____ in a sentence. For example, _____.

I know that the word _____ means _____.

We are unfamiliar with the word _____.

We recognize the word _____, but we would benefit from a review of what it means and how to use it.

We think _____ means _____.

Building Concepts

 DEVELOP UNDERSTANDING

Complete the organizer to build your knowledge of the concept.

nutrition *(noun)*

Example Sentence

Schools are thinking more about students' **nutrition** by offering breakfast, serving lunches with less fat, and switching to more **nutritious** choices in vending machines.

Synonyms		Word Family
Everyday:	Precise:	• nutrition *(noun)*
• _____	• _____	• nutritious *(adjective)*
• _____	• _____	• nutritional *(adjective)*

Meaning	Essential Characteristics
the process of eating the _____ you need to _____ and be _____	• food that is good for your _____ • the right _____ of food to grow well

Examples	Non-Examples
• snacking on raw vegetables • _____	• eating a donut for breakfast on a school day • _____

Write About It

Teens who are not worried about **nutrition** often _____ _____ and _____,
even on school days. One consequence is that they _____
_____

 BUILD KNOWLEDGE

Read and respond to the Data File (*Issues*, p. 15). Use the frames to discuss ideas with your group.

(*Issues*, p. 15)

Language to FACILITATE DISCUSSION

I choose _____.

I select _____.

1. One finding that caught my attention was _____ because _____.

2. One statistic that didn't surprise me at all was _____ because _____.

Words to Know

BUILD WORD KNOWLEDGE

Rate your word knowledge. Then discuss word meanings and examples with your group.

Language to COMPARE

Our example is similar to _____'s group's.

		① Don't Know	② Recognize	③ Familiar	④ Know

Words to Know	Meanings	Examples
1 **appealing** *adjective* ① ② ③ ④	likeable or _____	I find talking on the phone more **appealing** than _____ because talking is more personal. One food that is very **appealing** to me is _____ because _____
2 **ban** *noun* ① ② ③ ④	an order that says something is _____ _____	The students at my school will _____ _____ if the principal pushes for a **ban** on cell phone use. The school dress code includes a **ban** on _____
3 **epidemic** *noun* ① ② ③ ④	a sudden outbreak of a _____ or _____ _____ that spreads quickly	The high amount of _____ makes it seem as if we are suffering from an **epidemic** of bad behavior. As a result of the _____ **epidemic** at school, many students _____ _____ _____
4 **trend** *noun* ① ② ③ ④	a general _____ in which a situation is _____	I dislike the current **trend** of people using _____ _____ more often. At our school, wearing _____ _____ is a **trend** this year.

Language to FACILITATE DISCUSSION

I've never seen or heard the word _____.

I recognize the word _____ but need to learn how to use it.

I can use _____ in a sentence. For example, _____.

I know that the word _____ means _____.

We are unfamiliar with the word _____.

We recognize the word _____, but we would benefit from a review of what it means and how to use it.

We think _____ means _____.

Academic Discussion
Should schools ban unhealthy food?

BRAINSTORM IDEAS
Briefly record at least two ideas in each column using everyday English.

Agree	Disagree
• junk food makes teens gain weight	• most students are mature
•	•
•	•
•	•

ANALYZE LANGUAGE
Complete the chart with precise words to discuss and write about the topic.

Everyday	Precise
bad for you *(adjective)*	damaging,
very hungry *(adjective)*	famished,
eat *(verb)*	consume,

MAKE A CLAIM
Rewrite an idea using the frame and precise words. Then prepare to elaborate verbally.

Frame: I think that schools (should/should not) ban unhealthy foods because students (are/are not) capable of _____ (**verb + –ing:** making, deciding, spending, selecting)

Response: _____

_____

_____

_____

Language to ELABORATE

For example, _____.

I know this because _____.

EXCHANGE IDEAS
Listen attentively, restate, and record your partner's idea.

Classmate's Name	Idea

Language to RESTATE

So what you're saying is that _____.

Yes, that's right.

No, not really. What I meant was _____.

Ten-Minute Response

A **ten-minute response** uses academic register. It begins with a well-stated **claim**, followed by **two detail sentences** that elaborate with relevant examples and precise words.

PRESENT IDEAS

Listen attentively and take notes. Then indicate if you agree (+) or disagree (−).

Language to AGREE/DISAGREE

I (agree/don't agree) with _____'s idea.

Classmate's Name	Idea	+/−

Prompt	Should schools ban unhealthy food? Write a ten-minute response that states and supports your claim.

ELABORATE IN WRITING

Work with the teacher to write a ten-minute response in academic register.

Language to COLLABORATE

What should we write? We could put _____.

What do you think? We could also write _____.

Okay. Let's write _____.

I think that schools should ban unhealthy foods because students are not capable of changing harmful eating habits without help. For example, even when parents tell kids that junk food is _____ they continue to _____

_____

As a result, many students can _____

_____

Work with a partner to write a ten-minute response in academic register.

I think that schools _____ ban unhealthy foods because students _____ capable of _____

_____

For example, many students who _____

_____

_____

As a result, students _____

_____

_____

Words to Go

Language to LISTEN ACTIVELY

What example did you select? I selected _____.

What example did you add? I added _____.

BUILD WORD KNOWLEDGE

Complete the meanings and examples for these high-utility academic words.

Words to Go	Meanings	Examples
prevent pre•vent *verb*	to _____ something from happening	When I ride a bike, I _____ _____ to **prevent** accidents.
prevention pre•ven•tion *noun*	the act of _____ something from _____	If Maya becomes school president, she'll fight for the **prevention** of _____ _____

DISCUSS & WRITE EXAMPLES

Discuss your response with a partner. Then complete the sentence in writing.

In my opinion, the best way to **prevent** falling behind on homework is to _____ _____ because _____

Write your response and read it to a partner. Listen and record a new idea.

I believe that more education about good nutrition will aid in the _____

of _____

BUILD WORD KNOWLEDGE

Complete the meaning and examples for this high-utility academic word.

Word to Go	Meaning	Examples
indicate in•di•cate *verb*	to _____ or _____ something	Scoring well on a test **indicates** that someone _____ The crowd **indicated** that it enjoyed the performance by _____ _____

DISCUSS & WRITE EXAMPLES

Discuss your response with a partner. Then complete the sentence in writing.

Good listeners **indicate** that they are paying attention by _____

Write your response and read it to a partner. Listen and record a new idea.

_____

might _____ that a student is not getting enough sleep.

Classmate's Name	Idea for *Prevent/Prevention*	Idea for *Indicate*

Section Shrink

BUILD FLUENCY

Read the introduction and Section 1 of "Food Fight" (*Issues*, pp. 16–17).

IDENTIFY KEY IDEAS & DETAILS

Take turns asking and answering questions with a partner. Then write brief notes.

Discussion Frames	Text Notes
Q: What is the **key idea** of this section? **A:** The **key idea** of this section is _____ .	• junk food at school is connected to _____
Q: What are the **most important details** in this section? **A:** (One/Another) **important detail** in this section is _____ . **A:** Perhaps the **most important detail** in this section is _____ .	• _____ decreases childhood obesity • junk food at school can cause students to _____ each year • when schools banned junk food, _____ students became _____

CONDENSE IDEAS

Paraphrase a sentence from the text by keeping important topic words and replacing key words and phrases with synonyms.

Source Text	Key Words & Phrases → Synonyms		Paraphrasing
"Studies indicate that snacking on junk food in school adds up to about 14 extra pounds per child per school year" (Rodriguez 17).	Studies indicate snacking on junk food adds up to	→ → → → →	Research show _____ unhealthy snacks causes students to	Research shows that _____ unhealthy snacks at school causes students to _____ about 14 pounds per year.

IDENTIFY PRECISE WORDS

Review Section 1 and your *Portfolio* (pp. 28–35) to identify words for your summary.

Domain-Specific Topic Words	High-Utility Academic Words
• nutritious • •	• motivates • •

Words to Go

BUILD WORD KNOWLEDGE

Complete the meanings and examples for this high-utility academic word.

Word to Go	Meanings	Examples
available a•vail•a•ble *adjective*	_____ to get or be used; unoccupied or not _____	Libraries often have computers **available** so students can _____ I am not **available** on Saturday night because I have plans to _____ _____

DISCUSS & WRITE EXAMPLES

Discuss your response with a partner. Then complete the sentence in writing.

In my opinion, a student lounge should be **available** at our school because students need a

place to _____

Write your response and read it to a partner. Listen and record a new idea.

On weekends, I am often _____ to _____

_____

BUILD WORD KNOWLEDGE

Complete the meanings and examples for these high-utility academic words.

Words to Go	Meanings	Examples
impact im•pact *noun*	the _____ of one thing on another	_____ _____ had a great **impact** on Keisha's grades.
impact im•pact *verb*	to have an effect on _____	I am worried that this unexpected storm will impact _____ _____

DISCUSS & WRITE EXAMPLES

Discuss your response with a partner. Then complete the sentence in writing.

Watching less television on school nights can have a positive _____

on a student's _____

Write your response and read it to a partner. Listen and record a new idea.

A major injury to a star player could **impact** the team's chance of _____

_____

Classmate's Name	Idea for *Available*	Idea for *Impact*

Section Shrink

BUILD FLUENCY

Read Section 2 of "Food Fight" (*Issues*, pp. 17–18).

IDENTIFY KEY IDEAS & DETAILS

Take turns asking and answering questions with a partner. Then write brief notes.

Discussion Frames	Text Notes
Q: What is the **key idea** of this section? **A:** The **key idea** of this section is _____.	• a ban on _____ can have a negative _____
Q: What are the **most important details** in this section? **A:** (One/Another) **important detail** in this section is _____. **A:** Perhaps the **most important detail** in this section is _____.	• students don't learn to make _____ choices • vending machines keep students from being _____ • money from vending machines funds _____ _____

CONDENSE IDEAS

Paraphrase a sentence from the text by keeping important topic words and replacing key words and phrases with synonyms.

Source Text	Key Words & Phrases → Synonyms		Paraphrasing
"Food sales also have a major financial impact for many schools" (Rodriguez 18).	Food sales → major → financial → impact →	Selling snacks _____ economic _____	Selling snacks also has a _____ financial _____ for many schools.

IDENTIFY PRECISE WORDS

Review Section 2 and your *Portfolio* (pp. 36–37) to identify words for your summary.

Domain-Specific Topic Words	High-Utility Academic Words
• healthy choices • •	• options • •

Words to Go

Language to LISTEN ACTIVELY

What example did you select? I selected _____.

What example did you add? I added _____.

BUILD WORD KNOWLEDGE

Complete the meaning and examples for this high-utility academic word.

Word to Go	Meaning	Examples
restrict re•strict *verb*	to _____ the size, amount, or range of something	School rules often **restrict** students' _____ Some parents **restrict** the amount of time teens spend _____

DISCUSS & WRITE EXAMPLES

Discuss your response with a partner. Then complete the sentence in writing.

Many nutrition experts want a law that **restricts** the (amount/use/size)

_____ of _____

Write your response and read it to a partner. Listen and record a new idea.

If the principal _____ what students listen to at school dances, many

students will _____

BUILD WORD KNOWLEDGE

Complete the meaning and examples for this high-utility academic word.

Word to Go	Meaning	Examples
select se•lect *verb*	to pick out or _____	English teachers try to **select** readings that relate to their students' _____ You should try several _____ _____ before **selecting** one to purchase.

DISCUSS & WRITE EXAMPLES

Discuss your response with a partner. Then complete the sentence in writing.

My parents let me **select** what we would have for dinner on my birthday, so I chose

_____ because _____

Write your response and read it to a partner. Listen and record a new idea.

On social media sites, many teens _____ friends based on the

_____ they enjoy.

Classmate's Name	Idea for *Restrict*	Idea for *Select*

Close Reading

BUILD FLUENCY
Read Section 3 of "Food Fight" (*Issues*, pp. 19–20).

IDENTIFY KEY IDEAS & DETAILS
Take turns asking and answering questions with a partner. Then write brief notes.

Discussion Frames	Text Notes
Q: What is the **key idea** of this section? **A:** The **key idea** of this section is _____.	• people disagree about who should make food _____ for students
Q: What are the **most important details** in this section? **A:** (One/Another) **important detail** in this section is _____. **A:** Perhaps the **most important detail** in this section is _____.	• some think the government because so many children are _____ • some think _____ should teach healthy _____ • some think students would make _____ choices if they knew more about _____

RESPOND WITH EVIDENCE
Use the frame and evidence from the text to construct a formal written response.

1. According to the text, how does unhealthy food at school impact students' health?

   According to the text, unhealthy food at school can cause students to _____

   _____

   The impacts on students' health include an increase in _____

   and _____

Use the frame to analyze the author's word choice.

2. Why does the author use the word *battleground* on page 16 to describe a teen's body?

   The author uses the word *battleground* (literally/figuratively) _____

   to describe a teen's body because the fight about _____

   is based on _____

IDENTIFY PRECISE WORDS
Review Section 3 and your *Portfolio* (pp. 38–39) to identify words for your summary.

Domain-Specific Topic Words	High-Utility Academic Words
• health crises • •	• consequences • •

Academic Discussion

How can schools promote students' health?

BRAINSTORM IDEAS

Briefly record at least two ideas in each column using everyday English.

Physical Activity	Nutrition
• after-school running club	• serving seasonal fresh fruit at lunch
•	•
•	•
•	•

ANALYZE LANGUAGE

Complete the chart with precise words to discuss and write about the topic.

Everyday	Precise
good for you *(adjective)*	nourishing,
bad for you *(adjective)*	deep-fried,
something active *(noun)*	movement,

MAKE A CLAIM

Rewrite an idea using the frame and precise words. Then prepare to elaborate verbally.

Frame: One way schools can promote students' health is by _____ (**verb + –ing:** offering, providing increasing, banning)

Response: _____

_____

_____

_____

_____

Language to ELABORATE

For example, _____.

I know this because _____.

EXCHANGE IDEAS

Listen attentively, restate, and record your partner's idea.

Classmate's Name	Idea

Language to RESTATE

So what you're saying is that _____.

Yes, that's right.

No, not really. What I meant was _____.

Ten-Minute Response

A **ten-minute response** uses academic register. It begins with a well-stated **claim,** followed by **two detail sentences** that elaborate with relevant examples and precise words.

PRESENT IDEAS

Listen attentively and take notes. Then indicate if you agree (+) or disagree (–).

Classmate's Name	Idea	+/–

Prompt	How can schools promote students' health? Write a ten-minute response that states and supports your claim.

ELABORATE IN WRITING

Work with the teacher to write a ten-minute response in academic register.

Language to COLLABORATE

What should we write? We could put _____.

What do you think? We could also write _____.

Okay. Let's write _____.

> One way schools can promote students' health is by requiring students to take
> PE classes every day. For example, a required fitness class exposes students to a
> variety of interesting _____
> and challenging _____
> As a result, many students find activities they _____ and
> learn to _____
> _____

Work with a partner to write a ten-minute response in academic register.

> One way schools can promote students' health is by _____
> _____
> _____
> For example, schools should serve far more _____
> students enjoy such as _____ and much less deep-fried and
> _____ foods such as _____
> As a result, students will be _____ and less likely to
> become _____

Analyze a Speech

▶ **BUILD KNOWLEDGE**

Watch the speech "The First Lady Announces New School Wellness Standards."
Use the frames to discuss ideas with your partner.

1. Something important I learned was _____.

2. I appreciated how Michelle Obama _____ in her speech.

✎ **LISTEN & TAKE NOTES**

Watch the speech again. Listen closely and complete the outline.

I. First Lady Michelle Obama launched a program called _____

_____

   A. It tries to make students healthier by increasing _____

      and improving _____

II. Obama's first announcement is about new _____

_____

   A. Schools will _____ ads for _____

_____

   B. A White House summit on food marketing encouraged companies to _____

_____

_____

III. The second announcement is about schools _____ their

  breakfast programs.

   A. Almost 9 million kids will start their school days with a _____

    breakfast.

     i. Students who do so score 17.5 percent better on _____

       and they also _____

IV. Making sure kids are healthy is _____

_____

  It benefits the country because having _____ workers improves

  the economy.

Language to COMPARE
What stood out for me was _____.
I especially noted the fact that _____.
My reaction was similar to _____'s. I was also (impressed/surprised) by _____.

Close Viewing & Listening

Making Inferences
To make **inferences**, readers combine evidence from the text with their prior knowledge to figure out something the author has not directly stated.

IDENTIFY KEY IDEAS & DETAILS
Use the frames to make inferences and analyze key details.

1. Before making the two announcements, why does Michelle Obama talk about previous successes?

   Michelle Obama first talks about previous successes because she wants to show how

   Let's Move is already affecting children in _____ ways.

   Obama wants to make her audience think the two new announcements will also

   be _____

2. What are two reasons for expanding the school breakfast program?

   One reason for expanding the school breakfast program is that "millions of

   students" _____

   _____

   Another reason for expanding the program is that many of the students who qualify for free

   breakfast don't participate because they feel _____

   _____

ANALYZE CRAFT & STRUCTURE
Use the frames to analyze the author's language choices.

3. What is the effect of Obama using the pronoun *we* in this sentence: "Because I think we can all agree that our classrooms should be healthy places where kids are not bombarded with ads for junk food"?

   The effect of Obama using *we* is that she makes the audience feel included in the

   decision to _____

   _____

4. Obama says "by contrast, our kids see an average of just one ad a week for healthy products like water, fruits, and vegetables. Just one." Why does she repeat *just one*?

   Obama repeats *just one* because she wants to emphasize that children see very

   few _____

   such as _____ and _____

   She also wants to let her audience know that this adds to the problem of

   _____

Words to Go

BUILD WORD KNOWLEDGE

Complete the meaning and examples for this high-utility academic word.

Word to Go	Meaning	Examples
implement im•ple•ment *verb*	to _____ a plan or action into effect	Our student council **implemented** a _____ to assist new students during their first few weeks. On the first day of class, teachers **implement** rules about deadlines and _____

DISCUSS & WRITE EXAMPLES

Discuss your response with a partner. Then complete the sentence in writing.

I was upset when my parents **implemented** new rules about _____

_____

Write your response and read it to a partner. Listen and record a new idea.

My English teacher had to _____ a new policy for _____

_____ because so many students were

_____

BUILD WORD KNOWLEDGE

Complete the meaning and examples for this high-utility academic word.

Word to Go	Meaning	Examples
eliminate e•lim•i•nate *verb*	to completely _____ of something	Schools need to **eliminate** _____ _____ from vending machines. I recently **eliminated** songs by _____ on my playlist because I prefer other musicians like _____

DISCUSS & WRITE EXAMPLES

Discuss your response with a partner. Then complete the sentence in writing.

When I revised my paper, I **eliminated** _____ to improve my grade.

Write your response and read it to a partner. Listen and record a new idea.

My grandmother was _____ years of clutter from her garage, so I

helped her _____

Classmate's Name	Idea for *Implement*	Idea for *Eliminate*

Close Reading

BUILD FLUENCY
Read the text "The First Lady Announces New School Wellness Standards"
(*Issues*, pp. 21–23).

IDENTIFY KEY IDEAS
Take turns asking and answering the question with a partner. Then write brief notes.

Discussion Frames	Text Notes
Q: What is the **key idea** of this text? **A:** The **key idea** of this text is _____.	• schools should help students be healthy by banning _____ and providing _____

RESPOND WITH EVIDENCE
Use the frame and evidence from the text to construct a formal written response.

1. In addition to positively affecting their health, how will expanding the school breakfast program help students?

Expanding the school breakfast program will help students by improving their

_____

For example, children who eat a healthy breakfast have fewer discipline problems and

_____

Use the frame to analyze the author's word choice.

2. What is the meaning of the word *strides* on page 22? What context clue helped you determine the meaning?

The meaning of the word *strides* is _____

One context clue that helped me determine the meaning is that Obama uses the word

_____ as a synonym for *strides* in the next sentence.

Use the frame to analyze the author's craft and structure.

3. Obama often begins her sentences with the words *and*, *so*, and *because*. How does this affect the tone of the speech?

Beginning sentences with *and*, *so*, and *because* affects the tone of the speech by making it feel

more _____ and less _____

IDENTIFY PRECISE WORDS
Review Text 2 and your *Portfolio* (pp. 40–45) to identify words for your summary.

Domain-Specific Topic Words	High-Utility Academic Words
• wellness • •	• transformed • •

Student Writing Model

Academic Writing Type

A **formal written summary** is a type of informative writing. It provides an objective overview of the topic and important details from an informational text. The writer credits the author, but writes original sentences using precise topic words. A summary does not include the writer's personal opinions.

A. The **topic sentence** includes the text type, title, author, and topic.

B. Detail sentences include the important details from the summarized text.

C. The **concluding sentence** restates the author's conclusion in the writer's own words.

D. Transition words or phrases help the reader identify the most important details.

ANALYZE TEXT STRUCTURE

Read this student model to analyze the elements of a formal summary.

> **A**
>
>   In the magazine article titled "Game On or Game Over?," Oscar Gomez investigates the topic of how video games affect teens. First, Gomez reports that teens can become addicted to video games. The author also notes that video game advocates claim that video games can improve coordination and prepare people for certain professions.
>
> **B**
>
> In addition, he describes how critics of video games argue that they can make players less social, expose them to violent images, and lead to more aggressive behavior. Finally, Gomez concludes that as the debate over video games continues, both children and adults disagree
>
> **C**
>
> about the best way to make sure the influence of video games is beneficial to players.

MARK & DISCUSS ELEMENTS

Mark the summary elements and use the frames to discuss them with your partner.

1. **Number (1–4) the four elements of the topic sentence.**
   The topic sentence includes the _____.

2. **Draw a box around three transition words or phrases.**
   One transition (word/phrase) is _____. Another transition (word/phrase) is _____.

3. **Underline three important details.** *One important detail in this summary is _____.*

4. **Circle four citation verbs.** *One citation verb that the writer uses is _____.*

5. **Star four precise topic words and check four high-utility academic words.**
   An example of a (precise topic word/high-utility academic word) is _____.

Nouns & Pronouns to Credit an Author

Guidelines to Credit an Author

Topic Sentence: State the author's full name.
1st Important Detail: State the author's last name.
2nd Important Detail: Use the term *author, writer,* or *researcher.* For a speech, use *speaker.*
3rd Important Detail: Use the pronouns *he* or *she.*
Concluding Sentence: Use the author's last name.

IDENTIFY NOUNS & PRONOUNS

Read the summary and circle the nouns and pronouns that credit the author.

> In the speech titled "The First Lady Announces New School Wellness Standards," Michelle Obama discusses the importance of nutrition and physical activity for students. First, Obama points out that new guidelines have increased the amount of fruits, vegetables, whole grains, and lean protein in school lunches. The speaker also reports that new rules will ban junk food ads in schools. In addition, she explains that the breakfast program will grow to reach almost 9 million students. Finally, Obama concludes that better nutrition for students will lead to healthier adults who can work more productively, which will benefit the economy.

TAKE NOTES

Identify the nouns and pronouns to credit the author in the student model. Then write the nouns and pronouns you will use for your formal summary of Text 1.

Summary Sentence	Model Noun/Pronoun	Your Noun/Pronoun
Topic Sentence		
1st Detail		
2nd Detail		
3rd Detail		
Concluding Sentence		

Citation Verbs

Noun/Pronoun	Citation Verbs	Summary
(Author's full name)	explores: thinks carefully about causes or results discusses: considers different opinions about something investigates: tries to find out the truth presents: describes something to influence others examines: considers or studies something	(topic)
(Author's last name) *The author* *The writer* *He/She*	reports: gives only facts, not his or her opinions notes: mentions something especially interesting clarifies: makes something clearer by giving more detail suggests: gives an opinion or option emphasizes: says that something is especially important questions: asks whether something is true	that/how (important detail)
(Author's last name)	concludes: gives a final closing thought	that (conclusion)

IDENTIFY CITATION VERBS

Circle the citation verbs in the chart that you plan to use in your summary. Then complete each sentence with an appropriate citation verb.

1. Michelle Obama _____ two announcements for improving

   students' health.

2. She _____ how new guidelines will affect food ads children see.

3. Finally, Obama _____ that healthier students will become healthier

   adults, which will improve our country.

WRITE KEY IDEAS & DETAILS

Write three sentences about "Food Fight" using citation verbs.

1. _____   _____
   (noun/pronoun)   (citation verb)

   _____
   (topic)

   _____

2. _____   _____
   (noun/pronoun)   (citation verb)

   _____
   (important detail)

   _____

3. _____   _____
   (noun/pronoun)   (citation verb)

   _____
   (important detail)

   _____

Organize a Formal Summary

Prompt   Write a formal summary of "Food Fight."

Transitions to Connect Ideas	Examples
First, _____. _____ also _____. In addition, _____. Furthermore, _____. Finally, _____.	**First,** Gomez reports on research about how video games affect players' brains. **The author also** explains that video games can isolate young people or help them develop relationships. **Finally,** Gomez concludes that violence in video games is a particular concern for many people.

IDENTIFY TRANSITIONS

Review the transitions that writers use to add information and connect ideas. Then complete each sentence below with an appropriate transition.

1. _____ Obama explains new guidelines for food advertising.

2. _____ reports that the breakfast program will expand.

3. _____ Obama concludes that healthier students will benefit everyone.

PLAN KEY IDEAS & DETAILS

State the text information to write a topic sentence.

In the article titled (title) _____

(author's full name) _____

(citation verb: explores, examines, discusses) _____

(topic) _____

List three important details from the article using primarily your own words.

1. _____

_____

_____

2. _____

_____

_____

3. _____

_____

_____

Restate the author's conclusion in your own words.

_____

_____

_____

Write a Formal Summary

Prompt   Write a formal summary of "Food Fight."

WRITE A PARAGRAPH
Use the frame to write your topic sentence, detail sentences, and concluding sentence.

A

In the magazine article titled _____
(title)

_____ examines the _____
(author's full name)   (noun: issue, topic, subject)

of _____
(topic)

_____

B

First, _____   _____ that concerned
(author's last name)   (citation verb)

_____ began fighting against _____
(plural noun: individuals, people, citizens)   (evidence)

_____ about 10 years ago

when research showed a _____ problem of _____
(adjective: widespread, national, serious)   (evidence from text)

_____

The _____ also _____ that proponents
(noun: author, writer, researcher)   (citation verb)

of school junk food bans believe they would _____
(base verb: encourage, promote, support)

_____
(evidence from text)

_____ (he/she) _____ describes
(transition to connect ideas)

how opponents of junk food bans argue that these extreme

_____ would not help students make their own
(plural noun: restrictions, measures, guidelines)

_____ diet decisions, would leave many students feeling
(adjective: healthy, nutritious, nourishing)

_____ and would eliminate a way for schools to _____
(adjective: famished, starved, ravenous)   (evidence from text)

_____

C

_____   _____
(transition to connect ideas)   (author's last name)

concludes that as the debate over _____ continues,
(noun phrase)

children and adults alike disagree about the best way to _____
(base verb: make, improve, prevent)

_____
(evidence from text)

Rate Your Formal Summary

ASSESS YOUR DRAFT
Mark the elements in your formal summary.

1. Number (1–4) the four elements of the topic sentence.

2. Draw a box around three transition words or phrases.

3. Underline three important details.

4. Circle four citation verbs.

5. Star four precise topic words and check four high-utility academic words.

Scoring Guide
① Insufficient
② Developing
③ Sufficient
④ Exemplary

Rate your formal summary. Then have a partner rate it.

1. Does the topic sentence state the text type, title, author, and topic?	Self	① ② ③ ④
	Partner	① ② ③ ④
2. Did you paraphrase the most important details from the text?	Self	① ② ③ ④
	Partner	① ② ③ ④
3. Did you use transitions to connect ideas?	Self	① ② ③ ④
	Partner	① ② ③ ④
4. Did you include precise topic words and high-utility academic words?	Self	① ② ③ ④
	Partner	① ② ③ ④
5. Did you restate the author's conclusion using your own words?	Self	① ② ③ ④
	Partner	① ② ③ ④

REFLECT & REVISE
Record specific priorities and suggestions to help you and your partner revise.

(Partner) Positive Feedback: I appreciate how you (used/included/explained) _____

_____

(Partner) Suggestion: As you revise your summary, focus on (including/improving/
explaining) _____

(Self) Priority 1: My summary paragraph needs to (include/develop/explain) _____

_____

(Self) Priority 2: I plan to improve my summary by (adding/revising/checking) _____

_____

CHECK & EDIT
Use this checklist to proofread and edit your formal summary.

☐ Did you capitalize the title of the article and proper nouns?

☐ Did you put quotation marks around the title of the article?

☐ Do present-tense citation verbs end in *–s*?

☐ Is each sentence complete?

☐ Are all words spelled correctly?

Argument Speech

Prompt | What is one change our school cafeteria should make? Present a speech that states your claim and supports it.

BRAINSTORM IDEAS
Collaborate with a partner to write your claim and two reasons that support it.

My Claim: _____

_____

Reason 1: _____

_____

Reason 2: _____

_____

Counterclaim: _____

_____

SYNTHESIZE IDEAS
Take notes on evidence from the texts or your experience that supports your claim.

Evidence 1: _____

_____

Evidence 2: _____

_____

WRITE A SPEECH
With a partner, write a speech that states a claim and includes reasons and evidence. Use visuals or multimedia to clarify information and add interest.

We think that our school cafeteria should (add/change/offer/allow/improve) _____

_____

We believe this change will benefit students by _____

_____

Another major reason we suggest this improvement is that it will encourage students to

_____

_____

According to _____

data shows that _____

_____

Opponents might claim that _____

but we maintain that _____

For these reasons, we firmly believe that our school should consider improving the

school cafeteria by _____

_____

Present & Rate Your Speech

Maintaining Eye Contact
When presenting ideas during class or in a meeting, maintain **eye contact**. Look at your audience when you speak and make sure to look up from your notes every few seconds so that you look confident and engage your listeners.

PRESENT YOUR SPEECH
Present your speech to your small group. Make sure to maintain eye contact.

LISTEN & TAKE NOTES
Listen attentively and take notes.
Then indicate if you agree (+) or disagree (–).

Language to AFFIRM & CLARIFY
I agree with your claim that _____, but I wonder _____.
I have a question about _____.

Classmate's Name	Idea	+/–

ASSESS YOUR SPEECH
Use the Scoring Guide to rate your speech.

Scoring Guide	
① Insufficient	② Sufficient
③ Developing	④ Exemplary

1. Did you clearly state a claim?	① ② ③ ④
2. Did you include valid reasons and evidence to support your claim?	① ② ③ ④
3. Did you acknowledge a counterclaim and respond?	① ② ③ ④
4. Did you use appropriate eye contact?	① ② ③ ④
5. Did you include visual displays of multimedia to strengthen your claim?	① ② ③ ④

REFLECT
Write two ways you can improve your next speech.

Priority 1: I can improve my next speech by (including/changing) _____
_____

Priority 2: When I present my next speech, I will focus on (speaking/using) _____
_____

Issue 3 **Street Art**

LEARNING & LANGUAGE GOALS
Check your learning in this Issue against the objectives on pages 6–7.

Where's the line between art and vandalism?

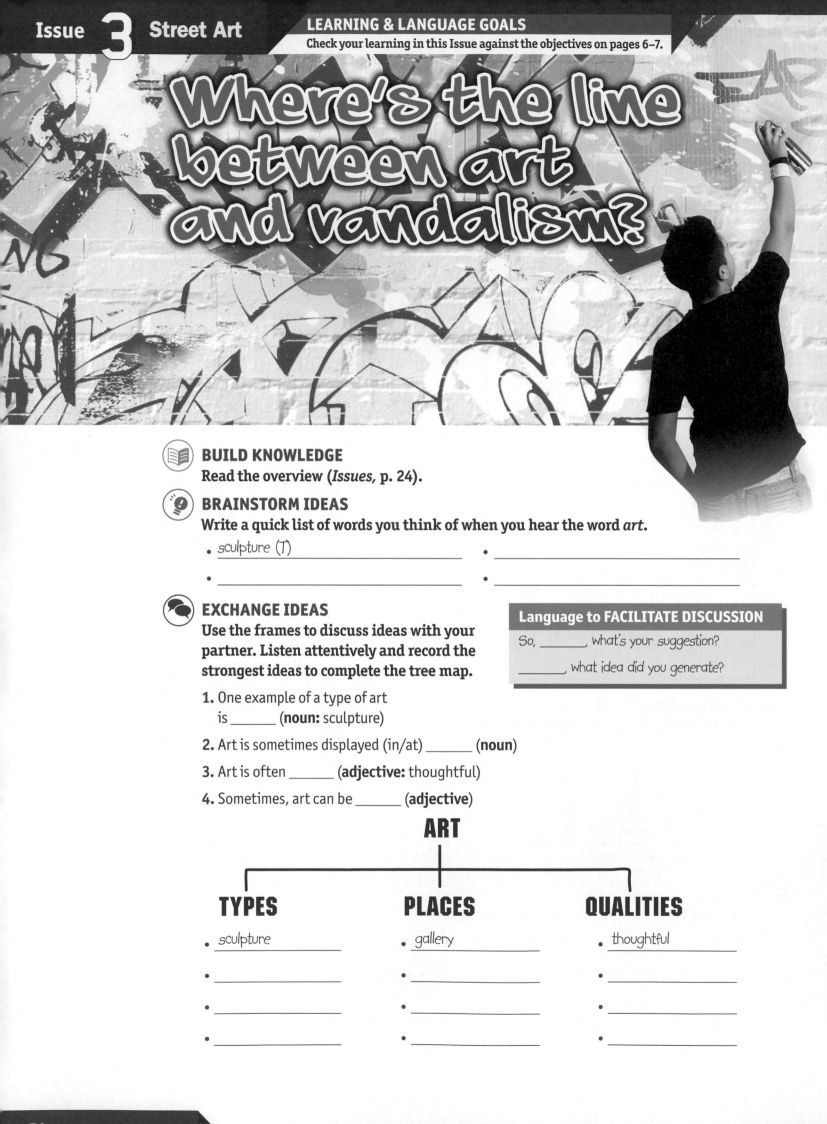

BUILD KNOWLEDGE
Read the overview (*Issues,* p. 24).

BRAINSTORM IDEAS
Write a quick list of words you think of when you hear the word *art*.

- sculpture (T) _____
- _____
- _____
- _____

EXCHANGE IDEAS
Use the frames to discuss ideas with your partner. Listen attentively and record the strongest ideas to complete the tree map.

1. One example of a type of art is _____ (**noun:** sculpture)

2. Art is sometimes displayed (in/at) _____ (**noun**)

3. Art is often _____ (**adjective:** thoughtful)

4. Sometimes, art can be _____ (**adjective**)

> **Language to FACILITATE DISCUSSION**
>
> So, _____, what's your suggestion?
>
> _____, what idea did you generate?

ART

TYPES	PLACES	QUALITIES
sculpture	gallery	thoughtful
_____	_____	_____
_____	_____	_____
_____	_____	_____

Words to Know

Language to COMPARE

Our group came up with a similar example.

BUILD WORD KNOWLEDGE

Rate your word knowledge. Then discuss word meanings and examples with your group.

	① Don't Know	② Recognize	③ Familiar	④ Know

Words to Know	Meanings	Examples
1 **artistic** *adjective* ① ② ③ ④	good at _____ or _____; done with _____ or _____	The movie director is **artistic** because she has a very imaginative way of showing _____ .... The way Eliana illustrated _____ _____ shows that she is very **artistic**.
2 **community** *noun* ① ② ③ ④	a _____ of _____ who live in an area; the area where a _____ of _____ live	Students can help their **communities** by volunteering to _____ _____ .... I admire our **community** because we all _____ _____
3 **express** *verb* ① ② ③ ④	to _____ what you are _____ _____ using words or actions	People often use emoticons to **express** feelings in _____ .... Some people can **express** what they are thinking using only _____
4 **vandal** *noun* ① ② ③ ④	someone who purposely _____ property	My neighbor thought that a **vandal** had broken his _____, but it was just _____ .... When I saw the _____ _____ I knew that **vandals** were at fault.

Language to FACILITATE DISCUSSION

I've never seen or heard the word _____.

I recognize the word _____ but need to learn how to use it.

I can use _____ in a sentence. For example, _____.

I know that the word _____ means _____.

We are unfamiliar with the word _____.

We recognize the word _____, but we would benefit from a review of what it means and how to use it.

We think _____ means _____.

Building Concepts

DEVELOP UNDERSTANDING
Complete the organizer to build your knowledge of the concept.

culture *(noun)*

Example Sentence

Listening to music that expresses our feelings about ourselves and our world is an important part of teen **culture**.

Synonyms		Word Family
Everyday:	Precise:	• culture *(noun)*
• _____	• _____	• cultural *(adjective)*
• _____	• _____	• culturally *(adverb)*

Meaning

the _____, beliefs, and

values of a _____

of people

Essential Characteristics

• ways of living that are

_____ by people

• how people live out their ideas in a

particular _____ or society

Examples

• foods commonly eaten in certain places

• _____

_____

_____

• _____

_____

_____

Non-Examples

• a habit of yours that no one else shares

• _____

_____

_____

• _____

_____

_____

Write About It

Some _____ is evidence of gang **culture**, but that's not always

true. In fact, much graffiti adds _____

and shows a community's **cultural** _____

BUILD KNOWLEDGE
Read and respond to the Data File (*Issues*, p. 25). Use the frames to discuss ideas with your group.

Language to FACILITATE DISCUSSION

I'd like to hear from _____.

I select _____.

1. One finding that caught my attention was _____ because _____.

2. One statistic that didn't surprise me at all was _____ because _____.

Words to Know

 BUILD WORD KNOWLEDGE

Rate your word knowledge. Then discuss word meanings and examples with your group.

Language to COMPARE

Our group came up with a similar example.

	① Don't Know	② Recognize	③ Familiar	④ Know

Words to Know	Meanings	Examples
1 **criticism** *noun* ① ② ③ ④	remarks that say what you think is _____ or _____ about something	The teacher's constructive **criticism** helped Sonja to correct _____ _____ in her writing.
		Students would like to offer **criticism** about _____ without getting into trouble.
2 **deface** *verb* ① ② ③ ④	to _____ or _____ the way something looks	Some students **deface** _____ by _____
		The teens were caught before they could **deface** _____ _____
3 **political** *adjective* ① ② ③ ④	having to do with _____ and how they are run	An effective **political** leader is someone who can _____ _____
		I'm not a very **political** person, but even I care about _____ _____
4 **target** *noun* ① ② ③ ④	someone or someplace that becomes the focus of an _____ or an _____, especially in a negative way	After several students _____, our school became the **target** of _____ _____
		The zoo's poor treatment of its animals has made it a **target** of _____ _____

Language to FACILITATE DISCUSSION

I've never seen or heard the word _____.

I recognize the word _____ but need to learn how to use it.

I can use _____ in a sentence. For example, _____.

I know that the word _____ means _____.

We are unfamiliar with the word _____.

We recognize the word _____, but we would benefit from a review of what it means and how to use it.

We think _____ means _____.

Academic Discussion

Is graffiti mostly art or vandalism?

BRAINSTORM IDEAS

Briefly record at least two ideas in each column using everyday English.

Art	Vandalism
• graffiti expresses culture of artist	• illegal in most places
•	•
•	•
•	•

ANALYZE LANGUAGE

Complete the chart with precise words to discuss and write about the topic.

Everyday	Precise
good at art *(adjective)*	creative,
make ugly *(verb)*	mar,
say *(verb)*	convey,

MAKE A CLAIM

Rewrite an idea using the frame and precise words. Then prepare to elaborate verbally.

Frame: Within my _____ (**noun:** family, group of friends, community, school), graffiti is mostly considered (art/ vandalism) because it _____ (**present-tense verb:** changes, encourages, causes, makes)

Response: _____

_____

_____

_____

_____

> **Language to ELABORATE**
>
> For instance, _____.
>
> The reason I know this is _____.

EXCHANGE IDEAS

Listen attentively, restate, and record your partner's idea.

Classmate's Name	Idea

> **Language to RESTATE**
>
> So what you're suggesting is that _____.
>
> Yes, that's right.
>
> Actually, what I meant was _____.

Ten-Minute Response

A **ten-minute response** uses academic register. It begins with a well-stated **claim**, followed by two **detail sentences** that elaborate with relevant examples and precise words.

PRESENT IDEAS
Listen attentively and take notes. Then indicate if you agree (+) or disagree (–).

Language to AGREE/DISAGREE

My experience is (similar to/ different from) _____'s.

Classmate's Name	Idea		+/–

Prompt	Is graffiti mostly art or vandalism? Write a ten-minute response that states and supports your claim.

ELABORATE IN WRITING
Work with the teacher to write a ten-minute response in academic register.

Language to COLLABORATE

Let's think about what to write. A good option might be _____.

What are your thoughts? We could also try _____.

Okay. Let's write _____.

Within my community, graffiti is mostly considered vandalism because it expresses dangerous or judgmental ideas. For example, graffiti is often used by _____ to _____ threats to a rival gang. As a result, that gang may _____ _____ which can _____ _____

Work with a partner to write a ten-minute response in academic register.

Within my group of friends, graffiti is mostly considered _____ because it _____ _____

For example, a lot of graffiti has been shown in _____ which shows that _____ are not the only people who create graffiti. As a result, most graffiti doesn't _____ _____

Words to Go

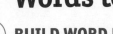

BUILD WORD KNOWLEDGE

Complete the meanings and examples for these high-utility academic words.

Words to Go	Meanings	Examples
remove re•move *verb*	to take something _____	When we moved to a new home, we had to **remove** the _____ that (was/were) left behind.
removal re•mov•al *noun*	the act of taking something _____	The **removal** of _____ _____ from the park made people upset.

DISCUSS & WRITE EXAMPLES

Discuss your response with a partner. Then complete the sentence in writing.

Removing _____ from our school activities would be a shame

because many students _____

Write your response and read it aloud to a partner. Listen and record a new idea.

A new school policy requires the _____ of any student who

_____

BUILD WORD KNOWLEDGE

Complete the meaning and examples for this high-utility academic word.

Word to Go	Meaning	Examples
represent rep•re•sent *verb*	to be a sign or mark that _____ something	At school, _____ _____ can **represent** your membership in a particular group. For many teens, turning 18 **represents** _____ _____

DISCUSS & WRITE EXAMPLES

Discuss your response with a partner. Then complete the sentence in writing.

In text messages, smiley faces and other emoticons **represent** _____

_____

Write your response and read it aloud to a partner. Listen and record a new idea.

An "A" on an assignment _____ a student's _____

_____

Classmate's Name	Idea for *Remove/Removal*	Idea for *Represent*

Section Shrink

BUILD FLUENCY
Read the introduction and Section 1 of "The Writing on the Wall" (*Issues,* pp. 26–28).

IDENTIFY KEY IDEAS & DETAILS
Take turns asking and answering questions with a partner. Then write brief notes.

Discussion Frames	Text Notes
Q: What is the author's **main idea**? **A:** The author's **main idea** is _____.	• many people consider graffiti to be _____ _____
Q: What are the **key details** in this section? **A:** (One/Another) **key detail** in this section is _____. **A:** Perhaps the **most important key detail** in this section is _____.	• graffiti has been a part of American culture since _____ • _____ use graffiti to mark _____ which can lead to violence • graffiti critics use _____ _____ theory" to explain their views

CONDENSE IDEAS
Read the three details. Then paraphrase key information into one sentence.

Text Detail 1	Text Detail 2	Text Detail 3
"Richard Condon . . . thinks graffiti has an impact just like a broken window" (Nguyen 28).	"One broken window in a community encourages vandals to break more windows" (Nguyen 28).	"Soon, the whole community becomes a target for littering, vandalism, and crime" (Nguyen 28).

Richard Condon feels illegal street art has the same _____

as a broken window because one broken window can _____

more broken windows, which can increase the rate of crime in _____

IDENTIFY PRECISE WORDS
Review Section 1 and your *Portfolio* (pp. 54–61) to identify words for your summary and response.

Domain-Specific Topic Words	High-Utility Academic Words
• gangs • •	• represent • •

Words to Go

Language to LISTEN ACTIVELY
What example did you add? I added _____.
What example did you record? I recorded _____.

 BUILD WORD KNOWLEDGE

Complete the meaning and examples for this high-utility academic word.

Word to Go	Meanings	Examples
identity i•den•ti•ty *noun*	a sense of _____; a feeling of _____ to a particular group	Vanessa's **identity** as a shy girl changed when she _____ I value my _____ because it is part of my **identity** as a(n) _____

 DISCUSS & WRITE EXAMPLES

Discuss your response with a partner. Then complete the sentence in writing.

In the United States, we _____

_____ as one way of showing our national **identity**.

Write your response and read it aloud to a partner.

My _____

_____ have helped to shape my _____

 BUILD WORD KNOWLEDGE

Complete the meanings and examples for these high-utility academic words.

Words to Go	Meanings	Examples
damage dam•age *verb*	to _____ something or someone	Water will **damage** a(n) _____ _____
damage dam•age *noun*	the _____ caused by something	After the _____ we examined the **damage** to our _____ _____

 DISCUSS & WRITE EXAMPLES

Discuss your response with a partner. Then complete the sentence in writing.

Lorenzo's reputation among his classmates was **damaged** when someone _____

_____

Write your response and read it aloud to a partner. Listen and record a new idea.

The _____ from _____

_____ can be a lifetime of poor health.

Classmate's Name	Idea for *Identity*	Idea for *Damage*

Section Shrink

BUILD FLUENCY

Read Section 2 of "The Writing on the Wall" (*Issues,* pp. 29–30).

IDENTIFY KEY IDEAS & DETAILS

Take turns asking and answering questions with a partner. Then write brief notes.

Discussion Frames	Text Notes
Q: What is the author's **main idea**? **A:** The author's **main idea** is _____.	• graffiti artists believe their work is _____ _____
Q: What are the **key details** in this section? **A:** (One/Another) **key detail** in this section is _____. **A:** Perhaps the **most important key detail** in this section is _____.	• the Mission District in _____ is an _____ • supporters say that graffiti is a _____ crime • artist Barry McGee says that graffiti is _____, and better than _____

CONDENSE IDEAS

Read the three details. Then paraphrase key information into one sentence.

Text Detail 1	Text Detail 2	Text Detail 3
"They claim that it makes a neighborhood beautiful and gives the community a cultural identity" (Nguyen 29).	"For decades, the Mission District in San Francisco has been an open-air gallery for graffiti artists" (Nguyen 29).	"The Mission's graffiti appeals to tourists rather than driving them away" (Nguyen 29).

Graffiti artists believe that their art _____ to the cultural identity of

an area, such as the Mission District in San Francisco, which features _____

_____ that _____ tourists to the area.

IDENTIFY PRECISE WORDS

Review Section 2 and your *Portfolio* (pp. 62–63) to identify words for your summary and response.

Domain-Specific Topic Words	High-Utility Academic Words
• rebels • •	• appeals • •

Words to Go

 BUILD WORD KNOWLEDGE

Complete the meaning and examples for this high-utility academic word.

Word to Go	Meaning	Examples
interpret in•ter•pret *verb*	to determine the _____ of something	Please don't **interpret** my remarks to mean that I think _____ _____ A teacher might ask students to **interpret** _____ _____

 DISCUSS & WRITE EXAMPLES

Discuss your response with a partner. Then complete the sentence in writing.

My parents **interpreted** my silence about where I was going as a sign that they would not

_____

Write your response and read it aloud to a partner. Listen and record a new idea.

When my best friend walked right past me in the hall, I _____

(his/her) behavior to mean that (he/she) was _____

 BUILD WORD KNOWLEDGE

Complete the meaning and examples for this high-utility academic word.

Word to Go	Meaning	Examples
legal le•gal *adjective*	allowed by _____	_____ _____ is **legal** when you are accompanied by an adult. In our community, _____ _____ _____ is not **legal**.

 DISCUSS & WRITE EXAMPLES

Discuss your response with a partner. Then complete the sentence in writing.

I think the **legal** voting age is 18 because _____

_____

Write your response and read it aloud to a partner. Listen and record a new idea.

I believe that _____

should not be _____

Classmate's Name	Idea for *Interpret*	Idea for *Legal*

Close Reading

BUILD FLUENCY

Read Section 3 of "The Writing on the Wall" (*Issues*, pp. 30–31).

IDENTIFY KEY IDEAS & DETAILS

Take turns asking and answering questions with a partner. Then write brief notes.

Discussion Frames	Text Notes
Q: What is the author's **main idea**? **A:** The author's **main idea** is _____.	• people are trying to make distinctions between _____

Q: What are the **key details** in this section?
 	
A: (One/Another) **key detail** in this section is _____.
A: Perhaps the **most important key detail** in this section is _____.
	• cities like San Diego are _____
	  graffiti offenders
	
	• some _____are not part
	  of a _____ or crew
	
	• _____
	
	  encourage _____

RESPOND WITH EVIDENCE

Use the frame and evidence from the text to construct a formal written response.

1. What is the main concern of the San Diego Sheriff's office when it comes to arresting graffiti offenders? How do you know?

   The main concern of the San Diego Sheriff's office is to arrest graffiti offenders because

   they may be _____

   According to the text, Bill Miles notes that some taggers are not part of

   _____ and says that he _____ legal tagging.

Use the frame to analyze the author's use of language.

2. Why does the author use the phrase *draw the line* on page 30 to describe the actions of politicians?

   The author uses the phrase *draw the line* (literally/figuratively) _____

   to indicate the separation between _____

   and _____ The phrase is

   clever because it suggests actually _____ lines, as in graffiti.

IDENTIFY PRECISE WORDS

Review Section 3 and your *Portfolio* (pp. 64–65) to identify words for your summary and response.

Domain-Specific Topic Words	High-Utility Words
• crew	• protests
•	•
•	•

Academic Discussion

Should cities create mural zones for street artists?

BRAINSTORM IDEAS

Briefly record at least two ideas in each column using everyday English.

Agree	Disagree
• keep street artists out of trouble	• might encourage gang activity
•	•
•	•
•	•

ANALYZE LANGUAGE

Complete the chart with precise words to discuss and write about the topic.

Everyday	Precise
give *(verb)*	offer,
stop *(verb)*	deter,
get (people to) *(verb)*	persuade,

MAKE A CLAIM

Rewrite an idea using the frame and precise words. Then prepare to elaborate verbally.

Frame: In my opinion, cities (should/should not) create mural zones because they (will/will not) _____ (**present-tense verb:** encourage, reduce, develop, cause)

Response: _____

_____

_____

_____

Language to ELABORATE

For instance, _____.

The reason I know this is _____.

EXCHANGE IDEAS

Listen attentively, restate, and record your partner's idea.

Classmate's Name	Idea

Language to RESTATE

So what you're suggesting is that _____.

Yes, that's right.

Actually, what I meant was _____.

Ten-Minute Response

A **ten-minute response** uses academic register. It begins with a well-stated **claim**, followed by **two detail sentences** that elaborate with relevant examples and precise words.

PRESENT IDEAS
Listen attentively and take notes. Then write if you agree (+) or disagree (–).

Language to COMPARE IDEAS

My belief is (similar to/different from) _____'s.

Classmate's Name	Idea	+/–

Prompt Should cities create mural zones for street artists? Write a ten-minute response that states and supports your claim.

ELABORATE IN WRITING
Work with the teacher to write a ten-minute response in academic register.

Language to COLLABORATE

Let's think about what to write. A good option might be _____.

What are your thoughts? We could also try _____.

Okay. Let's write _____.

In my opinion, cities should not create mural zones because they will not deter gang graffiti in other parts of the city. For example, gangsters tag to _____

_____

while artists do so to _____

_____

As a result, gangsters will continue _____

_____ despite the availability of _____

Work with a partner to write a ten-minute response in academic register.

In my opinion, cities _____ create mural zones because

they _____ graffiti artists to see _____

_____

This is important because artists have _____

_____

As a result, the graffiti artists in a city can _____

_____

Language to LISTEN ACTIVELY

What example did you add? I added _____.

What example did you record? I recorded _____.

Words to Go

BUILD WORD KNOWLEDGE

Complete the meaning and examples for this high-utility academic word.

Word to Go	Meaning	Examples
border bor•der *noun*	the dividing _____ between two _____ or _____	The United States of America shares a **border** with _____ .... On our vacation, my family drove over the **border** into _____ so we could visit _____ _____

DISCUSS & WRITE EXAMPLES

Discuss your response with a partner. Then complete the sentence in writing.

While some states like Colorado have straight **borders**, others have **borders** that follow

natural features like _____

Write your response and read it aloud to a partner. Listen and record a new idea.

Many countries use _____

_____ to help protect their **borders**.

BUILD WORD KNOWLEDGE

Complete the meaning and examples for this high-utility academic word.

Word to Go	Meaning	Examples
chronicle chron•i•cle *verb*	to _____ events the way they _____ happened	The movie **chronicles** _____ _____ from beginning to end. .... The principal made us **chronicle** exactly what caused the _____ _____

DISCUSS & WRITE EXAMPLES

Discuss your response with a partner. Then complete the sentence in writing.

I wrote a report **chronicling** the events that led to _____

_____

Write your response and read it aloud to a partner. Listen and record a new idea.

In the past, Maria _____ her private thoughts in her

journal, but she stopped when _____

Classmate's Name	Idea for *Border*	Idea for *Chronicle*

Close Reading

READ THE TEXT

Read the poem "Graffiti on Christina Street" (*Issues*, pp. 32–33).

IDENTIFY KEY IDEAS & DETAILS

Use the frames to make inferences and analyze key details.

1. What does the poet compare?

The poet compares the _____ in Cardiff with

the _____ back home.

2. Why does the poet marvel at the sight of the graffiti in Cardiff?

The poet marvels at the sight of the graffiti in Cardiff because it shows _____

_____

In contrast, the graffiti back home is all about _____

_____

ANALYZE CRAFT & STRUCTURE

Analyzing Figurative Language

Figurative language is words and phrases whose meanings differ from their
literal interpretations. Authors often use figurative language to help readers
visualize what is happening.

Use the frames to analyze the poet's use of figurative language.

3. The poet writes of "the day when time stood still." What does the figurative phrase "time
stood still" emphasize about the effect of the graffiti in Cardiff?

The poet uses the figurative phrase "time stood still" to emphasize that the graffiti in Cardiff

made it seem like everything _____

because she was _____ at the differences between

_____

_____

ANALYZE THEME

Use the frames to analyze the poem's theme.

4. How do the poem's closing lines, "They would haunt us/Long after we left . . .," contribute to
the poem's theme, or overall message?

The lines "They would haunt us/Long after we left . . ." mean that the speaker never forgot that

life is _____

She wants the reader to understand that she continues to feel _____

_____

over the _____ in her homeland.

Analyze a Slideshow

▶ **BUILD KNOWLEDGE**

View the slideshow "Spirit of the Streets." Use the frames to discuss ideas with your partner.

1. In the photo of _____ I noticed _____.

2. The photo that appeals to me the (most/least) is _____ because _____.

✎ **VIEW & TAKE NOTES**

Watch the slideshow closely and complete the outline.

I. *The New York Times* presents 21 images of _____

   A. All of the images show graffiti in _____

II. Many of the pieces are part of special _____ established

   to _____ neighborhoods. Others are found in locations that are

   more like _____

   A. The Welling Court Mural Project in Queens, the Bushwick Collective in Brooklyn,

      and the Hunts Point Murals in the Bronx provide _____

      in neighborhoods that look _____

   B. Five Pointz and the Graffiti Hall of Fame attract _____, who

      come to see the graffiti and take pictures.

III. The artworks feature many different _____

   A. For example, some photos show _____

      Some just show _____

      _____

   B. Some works are three-dimensional sculptures, such as the one with _____

      _____

Language to COMPARE IDEAS
What stood out for me was _____.
I especially noted the fact that _____.
My reaction was similar to _____'s. I was also (impressed/surprised) by _____.

Close Viewing

IDENTIFY KEY IDEAS & DETAILS
Use the frames to make inferences and analyze key details.

1. What do you notice about the people in photos 8–10?

   The people in photos 8–10 are not _____
   _____

   This shows that the graffiti has become part of _____
   _____

ANALYZE CRAFT & STRUCTURE
Use the frame to analyze figurative language.

2. The caption for photo 5 says that the Welling Court Mural Project "packs the punch of a hidden, completely unexpected urban art gallery." What does the figurative phrase "packs the punch" emphasize about the project?

   The caption uses the figurative phrase "packs the punch" to emphasize that the project has a

   powerful _____, like a _____

> ### Analyzing Composition
> **Composition** is the way parts of a photograph or picture are arranged. It involves what photographers choose to include and leave out of an image and where they put the camera in relation to the subject.

Use the frames to analyze the slideshow's composition.

3. Why do the photographs in the slideshow often include the streets, sidewalks, cars, and buildings located near the graffiti?

   The photographs in the slideshow often include the streets, sidewalks, cars, and

   buildings located near the graffiti to emphasize that the graffiti is (a/an) _____
   _____

   and that people _____
   _____

4. What does the composition of the final photo communicate to viewers?

   The composition of the final photo includes a _____

   in front of a _____ Showing the creativity of the _____

   next to what is likely the result of a crime or neglect communicates to viewers the

   possibility of a conflict between the _____ of the people living in

   Hunts Point and the _____ of their lives.

Student Writing Model

Academic Writing Type

A **summary and response** provides an objective overview of the topic and important details from a text and then presents the writer's position on the issue.

A. The **summary** includes a topic sentence, detail sentences, and a concluding sentence.

B. The **response** includes a transitional sentence, a topic sentence that presents the writer's position, supporting details, and a final statement.

ANALYZE TEXT STRUCTURE

Read this student model to analyze the elements of a summary and response.

A

In the article "Food Fight," the author Dora Rodriguez explores the issues surrounding junk food in schools. Initially, Rodriguez explains that people first noted the impact about ten years ago, when research indicated that obesity in students was becoming an epidemic. The author continues to report that proponents of a junk food ban believe it will promote better nutrition and health. Additionally, she explains that critics think a ban will reduce choice and make fund-raising more difficult. Rodriguez concludes by stating that people disagree about what to do about junk food in schools.

B

Whether schools should ban junk food or not is a complex question. After analyzing the evidence presented in Rodriguez's article and my own experiences, it is clear that junk food has a number of negative impacts. One predictable harmful impact is that students are more likely to eat junk food if it is available. For example, one teacher states that when schools have deals with junk food companies, it sends the message that it is okay. Another common consequence noted in the article is the trend of weight gain. For instance, junk food can cause students to gain 14 pounds a year. These damaging impacts lead me to believe that schools should support efforts to restrict junk food.

MARK & DISCUSS ELEMENTS

Mark the summary and response elements. Then discuss them with your partner.

1. **Double underline the writer's position.** *The writer's position is _____.*

2. **Underline and label three reasons or pieces of evidence that support the writer's position with the letter *R* or *E*.** *One (reason/piece of evidence) is _____.*

3. **Draw a box around four transition words or phrases.** *One transition (word/phrase) is _____.*

4. **Circle four citation verbs in the essay.** *One citation verb is _____.*

5. **Star four precise topic words and check four high-utility academic words.**
   An example of a (precise topic word/high-utility word) is _____.

Precise Adjectives to Respond

Guidelines for Using Precise Adjectives to Respond

Precise adjectives help describe nouns more vividly and make your writing more interesting. Use a precise adjective in the transitional sentence of your summary and response essay.

Everyday Adjectives	Precise Adjectives
good	fair, appropriate, worthy, timely, wise
interesting	fascinating, intriguing, thought-provoking, provocative, controversial
hard	difficult, troubling, challenging, complex, complicated, perplexing
silly	absurd, preposterous, ridiculous
untrue	unfounded, groundless, baseless

WRITE PRECISE ADJECTIVES

Complete each transitional sentence with a precise adjective from the chart above.

1. Whether video games harm teens or not is (a/an) _____ question.

2. Whether schools should ban unhealthy food or not is (a/an) _____ question.

3. Whether school days should start later or not is (a/an) _____ question.

Answer each question with a transitional sentence that includes a precise adjective.

Frame: Whether _____ (noun) should _____ (verb phrase) or not is (a/an) _____ (precise adjective) question.

1. **Issue:** Should schools ban unhealthy food?

   Transitional Sentence: _____

   _____

2. **Issue:** Should schools use video games in classes?

   Transitional Sentence: _____

   _____

3. **Issue:** Should social media sites set a minimum age requirement of 12 years old?

   Transitional Sentence: _____

   _____

4. **Issue:** Should public schools force students to wear uniforms?

   Transitional Sentence: _____

   _____

5. **Issue:** Should students have to pass through metal detectors to get into school?

   Transitional Sentence: _____

   _____

Compound & Complex Sentences

Guidelines for Writing Compound & Complex Sentences

A **compound sentence** contains two or more independent clauses, each containing a subject and a predicate to express a complete thought. The independent clauses can be joined with these words: *for, and, nor, but, or, yet, so.*

A **complex sentence** contains an independent clause and one or more dependent clauses. A dependent clause cannot stand on its own as a sentence, and it often begins with a word or phrase such as *because, while, even though, since, until,* or *that.*

Presenting Reasons	Examples of Complex Sentences
One (beneficial/harmful) impact is how _____.	**One beneficial impact is how** adequate sleep improves students' grades.
It is important to note that _____.	**It is important to note that** a lack of sleep leads to health problems.
Presenting Evidence	**Examples of Compound Sentences**
To illustrate, _____.	**To illustrate,** schools with later start times have better attendance rates, and more students graduate.
For instance, _____.	**For instance,** students without enough sleep are prone to problems with their immune systems, so they get sick more often.

✏ PRESENT REASONS & EVIDENCE

Work with the teacher to write a reason and piece of evidence.

Claim: Schools should ban unhealthy foods.

Reason: One harmful impact is how _____

_____

Evidence: To illustrate, _____

and _____

Work with a partner to write a reason and piece of evidence.

Claim: Schools _____ use video games in classes.

Reason: It is important to note that _____

_____

Evidence: For instance, _____

_____

Work on your own to write a reason and piece of evidence.

Claim: Social media _____ have a lower minimum age requirement.

Reason: I am in favor of _____

_____

Evidence: For example, _____

_____

Organize a Summary & Response

Prompt Write a summary and response for "The Writing on the Wall."

Transitions to Organize Details	Examples
Initially, _____. *To begin with, _____.* *_____ continues to _____.* *Additionally, _____.* *Finally, _____.*	**To begin with,** the author reports that graffiti encourages vandalism. **The writer continues to** point out that neighborhoods can become targets for other crimes. **Additionally,** she notes that graffiti leads to violence. **Finally,** Nguyen concludes by stressing that graffiti artists should work within the legal system.

IDENTIFY TRANSITIONS

Review the transitions that writers use to organize details. Then complete the partial summary with appropriate transitions.

_____ the author explains that some people think graffiti

contributes to the deterioration of neighborhoods. _____ present

the views of graffiti artists who believe that their work is art. _____ she

reports that law enforcement is cracking down on graffiti offenders in certain states.

_____ Nguyen concludes by asking if graffiti artists can follow the law.

PLAN KEY IDEAS & DETAILS

State the text information to write a topic sentence for the summary.

In the article (title) _____ the author (author's full name)

_____ (citation verb: discusses, explores, examines) _____

issues surrounding the impacts of (topic) _____

List three important details from the article using primarily your own words.

1. _____

_____

2. _____

_____

3. _____

_____

Describe your position and write a topic sentence for the response.

After analyzing the evidence presented in (author's last name + '–s)

_____ article and my own _____ experiences,

it is _____ that graffiti has a number of (positive/negative)

_____ impacts on a community.

Write a Summary & Response

Prompt   Write a summary and response for "The Writing on the Wall."

✏️ **WRITE AN ESSAY**
Use the frame to write a two-paragraph summary and response.

A

In the article _____
(title)

the author _____ _____ issues
(author's full name)   (citation verb: discusses, explores, examines)

surrounding the impacts of _____
(topic)

Initially, _____ _____ the opposing
(author's last name)   (citation verb: describes, clarifies, emphasizes)

arguments about whether graffiti is truly artistic _____
(noun: expression, contribution, talent)

or merely _____ vandalism. The (author/writer)
(adjective: dangerous, destructive, damaging)

_____ continues to _____ that
(citation verb: report, state, point out)

opponents of graffiti _____ it to be a crime, and they think
(present-tense verb: view, perceive, consider)

it increases _____ in a neighborhood. _____
(noun: vandalism, violence, gang activity)   (transition to connect ideas)

(he/she) explains that graffiti _____
(plural noun: proponents, supporters, advocates)

_____ that murals can express a community's
(verb to express opinion: argue, maintain, contend)

_____
(noun phrase)

_____ concludes by _____ if graffiti
(Author's last name)   (verb + -ing: asking, questioning, wondering)

artists can create art within society's legal _____
(noun: system, boundaries, constraints)

B

Whether cities should _____ graffiti or not is a
(precise verb: permit, condone, prohibit, penalize)

_____ question. After analyzing the evidence presented in
(adjective: fascinating, complex, controversial)

_____ article and my own _____
(author's last name + 's)   (adjective: relevant, prior, recent, personal)

experiences, it is _____ that graffiti has a number of
(adjective: clear, obvious, apparent)

(positive/negative) _____ impacts on a community. One

(beneficial/harmful) _____ impact is how graffiti (improves/

damages) _____ _____ property.
(adjective: private, public, abandoned, neglected)

For example, the _____ on the _____
(precise noun)   (precise location)

_____ clearly _____ that graffiti can significantly
(precise verb: demonstrates, illustrates, proves)

_____ the appearance of a neighborhood. Another
(precise verb: improve, enhance, damage, ruin)

common consequence _____ in the article is the sense of
(past-tense citation verb)

_____ that _____ feel.
(noun: resentment, accomplishment, pride)   (plural noun: artists, residents, community members)

These _____ impacts lead me to believe that _____
(precise adjective)   (plural noun: legislators, citizens, police officers)

should support efforts to _____ graffiti.
(base verb: prevent, encourage, forbid)

Rate Your Summary & Response

ASSESS YOUR DRAFT

Rate your summary and response. Then have a partner rate it.

Scoring Guide
① Insufficient
② Developing
③ Sufficient
④ Exemplary

1. Does the summary topic sentence state the text type, title, author, and topic?	Self	① ② ③ ④
	Partner	① ② ③ ④
2. Did you paraphrase the most important details from the text?	Self	① ② ③ ④
	Partner	① ② ③ ④
3. Did you use transitions to introduce reasons or evidence?	Self	① ② ③ ④
	Partner	① ② ③ ④
4. Does your response clearly present your position?	Self	① ② ③ ④
	Partner	① ② ③ ④
5. Does your response include strong reasons and evidence?	Self	① ② ③ ④
	Partner	① ② ③ ④
6. Did you include precise topic words and high-utility academic words?	Self	① ② ③ ④
	Partner	① ② ③ ④
7. Did you conclude with a strong final statement that restates your position?	Self	① ② ③ ④
	Partner	① ② ③ ④

REFLECT & REVISE

Record specific priorities and suggestions to help you and your partner revise.

(Partner) Positive Feedback: I appreciate how you (used/included/explained) _____

_____

(Partner) Suggestion: As you revise your summary and response, focus on (including/

improving/explaining) _____

(Self) Priority 1: My summary and response needs to (include/develop/explain)

_____

(Self) Priority 2: I plan to improve my summary and response by (adding/revising/

checking) _____

CHECK & EDIT

Use this checklist to proofread and edit your summary and response.

☐ Did you capitalize the title of the article and proper nouns?

☐ Did you use commas appropriately in complex and compound sentences?

☐ Do present-tense citation verbs end in –*s*?

☐ Is each sentence complete?

☐ Are all words spelled correctly?

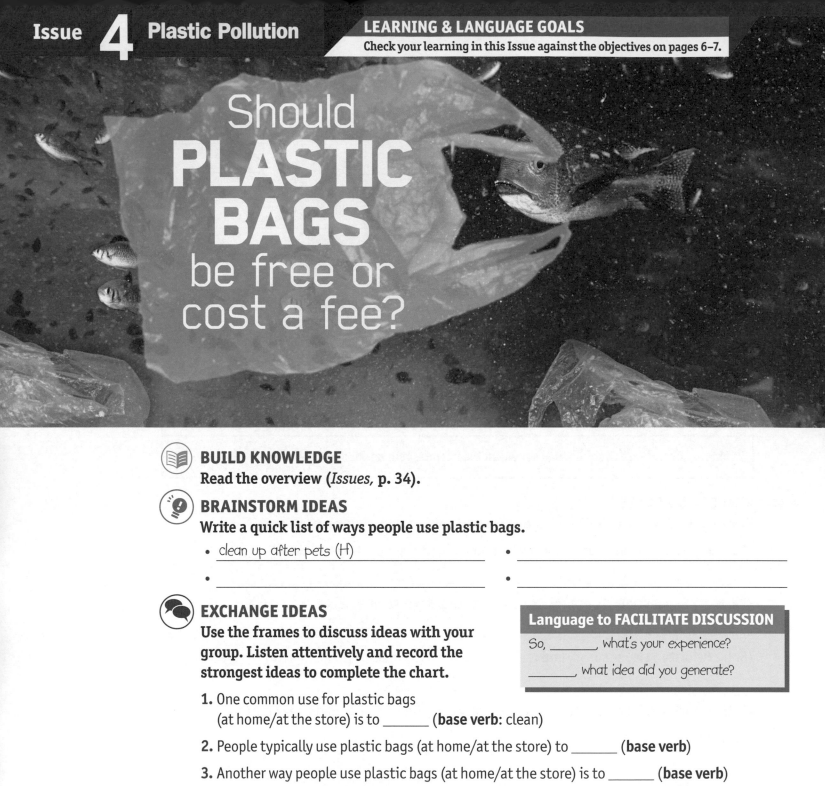

Should PLASTIC BAGS be free or cost a fee?

BUILD KNOWLEDGE
Read the overview (*Issues*, p. 34).

BRAINSTORM IDEAS
Write a quick list of ways people use plastic bags.

- clean up after pets (H)
- _____
- _____
- _____

EXCHANGE IDEAS
Use the frames to discuss ideas with your group. Listen attentively and record the strongest ideas to complete the chart.

Language to FACILITATE DISCUSSION

So, _____, what's your experience?

_____, what idea did you generate?

1. One common use for plastic bags (at home/at the store) is to _____ (**base verb:** clean)

2. People typically use plastic bags (at home/at the store) to _____ (**base verb**)

3. Another way people use plastic bags (at home/at the store) is to _____ (**base verb**)

4. People also might use plastic bags (at home/at the store) to _____ (**base verb**)

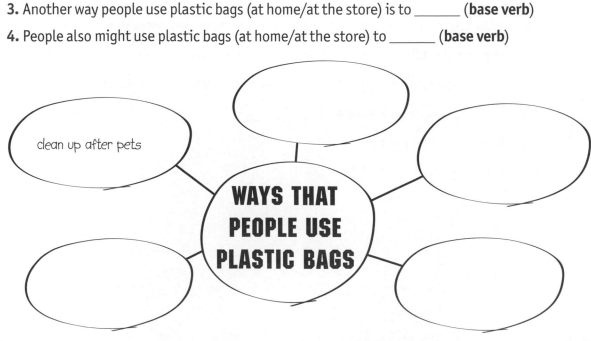

clean up after pets

WAYS THAT PEOPLE USE PLASTIC BAGS

Words to Know

BUILD WORD KNOWLEDGE

Rate your word knowledge. Then discuss word meanings and examples with your group.

		① Don't Know ② Recognize ③ Familiar ④ Know
Words to Know	**Meanings**	**Examples**
1 **dispose** *verb* ①②③④	to use something briefly and _____ _____	After the birthday party, we **disposed** of _____ _____ I need to clean out my closet and **dispose** of _____ _____
2 **legislation** *noun* ①②③④	a _____ or group of _____	Our town has **legislation** that prohibits _____ _____ One important piece of **legislation** the government passed is that _____ _____ _____
3 **litter** *verb* ①②③④	to leave _____ lying around	The mayor signed a law making it a crime to **litter** in _____ _____ Ellen got in trouble for **littering** when she _____ _____
4 **pollute** *verb* ①②③④	to use harmful materials that _____ or _____ the air, water, or soil	One way to **pollute** the air less is to _____ _____ Whenever you _____ _____ _____ you **pollute** the environment.

Building Concepts

 DEVELOP UNDERSTANDING
Complete the organizer to build your knowledge of the concept.

environment *(noun)*

Example Sentence

As an **environmentalist,** I'm concerned about litter on the street, as well as the impact of fossil fuels on the **environment** in general.

Synonyms		Word Family
Everyday:	Precise:	• environment *(noun)*
• _____	• _____	• environmental *(adjective)*
• _____	• _____	• environmentalist *(noun)*

Meaning	Essential Characteristics
the _____ surroundings of living things, such as the _____	• supports _____ • everything in a particular _____

Examples	Non-Examples
• breathing air • _____ _____ • _____ _____	• the Internet • _____ _____ • _____ _____

Write About It

The **environment** I live in contains many _____

and _____

I can care for the **environment** by _____

and _____

📖 **BUILD KNOWLEDGE**
Read and respond to the Data File (*Issues,* p. 35). Use the frames to discuss ideas with your group.

1. One finding that caught my attention is _____ because _____.

2. One statistic that didn't surprise me at all was _____ because _____.

Language to FACILITATE DISCUSSION

I'd like to hear from _____.

I select _____.

Words to Know

Language to COMPARE
Our group came up with a similar example.

 BUILD WORD KNOWLEDGE
Rate your word knowledge. Then discuss word meanings and examples with your group.

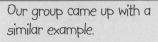

		① Don't Know	② Recognize	③ Familiar	④ Know

Words to Know	Meanings	Examples
1 **recycle** *verb* ①②③④	to put _____ objects through a process so they can be made into something _____	The specially marked bins at school encourage students to **recycle** _____ _____ **Recycling** paper products can _____ _____ _____
2 **retailer** *noun* ①②③④	people or businesses who _____ _____ to customers	The most successful **retailers** in my community sell _____ The new mall is attractive to **retailers** because it is _____ _____
3 **reuse** *verb* ①②③④	to use something _____ _____	Jerrod likes to **reuse** his lunch containers, which helps reduce _____ _____ One problem with **reusing** _____ is that they _____ _____
4 **tax** *noun* ①②③④	money paid to the _____ for public services, such as education and roads	The politician said the new **tax** would benefit our community by _____ _____ Residents fund the city's _____ _____ by paying **taxes**.

Language to FACILITATE DISCUSSION

I've never seen or heard the word _____.

I recognize the word _____ but need to learn how to use it.

I can use _____ in a sentence. For example, _____.

I know that the word _____ means _____.

We are unfamiliar with the word _____.

We recognize the word _____, but we would benefit from a review of what it means and how to use it.

We think _____ means _____.

Academic Discussion

Should cities outlaw plastic bags?

BRAINSTORM IDEAS

Briefly record at least two ideas in each column using everyday English.

Agree	Disagree
• they never biodegrade	• people choose bags they prefer
•	•
•	•
•	•

ANALYZE LANGUAGE

Complete the chart with precise words to discuss and write about the topic.

Everyday	Precise
trash *(noun)*	refuse,
make illegal *(verb)*	outlaw,
save *(verb)*	conserve,

MAKE A CLAIM

Rewrite an idea using the frame and precise words. Then prepare to elaborate verbally.

Frame: From my perspective, cities (should/should not) prohibit plastic bags because they are _____ (**adjective:** wasteful, convenient) and _____ (**adjective:** harmful, reusable)

Response: _____

_____

_____

_____

_____

> **Language to ELABORATE**
>
> For instance, _____.
>
> The reason I know this is _____.

EXCHANGE IDEAS

Listen attentively, restate, and record your partner's idea.

Classmate's Name	Idea

> **Language to RESTATE**
>
> So your opinion is that _____.
>
> Yes, that's right.
>
> Actually, what I meant was _____.

Ten-Minute Response

A **ten-minute response** uses academic register. It begins with a well-stated **claim,** followed by **two detail sentences** that elaborate with relevant examples and precise words.

PRESENT IDEAS
Listen attentively and take notes. Then indicate whether you agree (+) or disagree (−).

Language to AGREE/DISAGREE

I (agree/disagree) with _____'s opinion.

Classmate's Name	Idea	+/−

Prompt	Should cities outlaw plastic bags? Write a ten-minute response that states and supports your claim.

ELABORATE IN WRITING
Work with the teacher to write a ten-minute response in academic register.

Language to COLLABORATE

Let's think about what to write. A good option might be _____.

What are your thoughts? We could also try _____.

Okay. Let's write _____.

From my perspective, cities should not outlaw plastic bags because they are optional and useful. For example, many people choose to reuse plastic bags

to _____

and _____

As a result, people have a practical way to _____

_____

and streets have less _____

_____

Work with a partner to write a ten-minute response in academic register.

From my perspective, cities (should/should not) _____

prohibit plastic bags because they are _____

_____

For example, plastic bags _____

_____

As a result, the bags affect _____

by _____

_____

Words to Go

 BUILD WORD KNOWLEDGE

Complete the meanings and examples for this high-utility academic word.

Word to Go	Meanings	Examples
resource re•source *noun*	available land, water, and natural energy that can be _____ ; something used to _____	Oil is one **resource** that people use to _____ The science lab is equipped with many **resources,** such as _____

 DISCUSS & WRITE EXAMPLES

Discuss your response with a partner. Then complete the sentence in writing.

One use of natural **resources** that threatens the planet is _____

_____

Write your response and read it aloud to a partner. Listen and record a new idea.

My father says our family has to find the financial _____ to help

_____

 BUILD WORD KNOWLEDGE

Complete the meanings and examples for these high-utility academic words.

Words to Go	Meanings	Examples
support sup•port *verb*	to _____ with something or someone	My family **supports** the town's ban on _____ _____
supporter sup•por•ter *noun*	a person who _____ in someone or favors something	I would be a strong **supporter** of a new school policy to _____ _____

 DISCUSS & WRITE EXAMPLES

Discuss your response with a partner. Then complete the sentence in writing.

One requirement most students would not **support** is _____

_____

Write your response and read it aloud to a partner. Listen and record a new idea.

The school board voted to pass a ban on _____

but could not find enough _____

Classmate's Name	Idea for *Resource*	Idea for *Support/Supporter*

Section Shrink

BUILD FLUENCY
Read the introduction and Section 1 of "Ban It or Bag It?" (*Issues,* pp. 36–37).

IDENTIFY KEY IDEAS & DETAILS
Take turns asking and answering questions with a partner. Then write brief notes.

Discussion Frames	Text Notes
Q: What is the author's **main idea**? **A:** The author's **main idea** is _____.	• people have opinions for and against _____ _____
Q: What are the **key details** in this section? **A:** (One/Another) **key detail** in this section is _____. **A:** Perhaps the **most important key detail** in this section is _____.	• India, China, and San Francisco have _____ bans on _____ • plastic kills _____ and contaminates _____ • opponents of a ban feel that prohibiting bags takes away _____ _____

CONDENSE IDEAS
Paraphrase the first paragraph of Section 1 (*Issues,* p. 36–37). Keep important topic words and replace key words and phrases with synonyms.

Key Words & Phrases → Synonyms			
countries	→ nations	disposable	→ _____
implemented	→ _____	was	→ became
bans	→ rules against	pass legislation to ban	→ _____

Nations like India and China have already _____

rules against _____ bags, and San Francisco became the first US

city to _____ plastic bags in 2007.

IDENTIFY PRECISE WORDS
Review Section 1 and your *Portfolio* (pp. 78–85) to identify words for your argument.

Domain-Specific Topic Words	High-Utility Academic Words
• landfills • •	• account for • •

Words to Go

Language to LISTEN ACTIVELY

What example did you record? I recorded _____.

What example did you appreciate? I appreciated _____.

BUILD WORD KNOWLEDGE

Complete the meanings and examples for this high-utility academic word.

Word to Go	Meaning	Examples
consumer con•sum•er *noun*	someone who _____ or _____ products and services	Stores often try to attract **consumers** by _____ Many teenage **consumers** prefer to _____

DISCUSS & WRITE EXAMPLES

Discuss your response with a partner. Then complete the sentence in writing.

Consumers can spend less money if they _____

_____

Write your response and read it aloud to a partner. Listen and record a new idea.

As a _____ I appreciate when stores _____

_____

BUILD WORD KNOWLEDGE

Complete the meanings and examples for these high-utility academic words.

Words to Go	Meanings	Examples
produce pro•duce *verb*	to _____ something new	I would enjoy **producing** a video about _____ _____
production pro•duc•tion *noun*	the process of creating _____ _____	The **production** of more _____ can threaten the environment.

DISCUSS & WRITE EXAMPLES

Discuss your response with a partner. Then complete the sentence in writing.

It took Julia a long time to **produce** _____

_____

Write your response and read it aloud to a partner. Listen and record a new idea.

When I'm able to _____

I notice that my level of _____ is much better.

Classmate's Name	Idea for *Consumer*	Idea for *Produce/Production*

Section Shrink

BUILD FLUENCY

Read Section 2 of "Ban It or Bag It?" (*Issues*, pp. 37–39).

IDENTIFY KEY IDEAS & DETAILS

Take turns asking and answering questions with a partner. Then write brief notes.

Discussion Frames	Text Notes
Q: What is the author's **main idea**? **A:** The author's **main idea** is _____.	• plastic bags can have _____ such as _____
Q: What are the **key details** in this section? **A:** (One/Another) **key detail** in this section is _____. **A:** Perhaps the **most important key detail** in this section is _____.	• 14 million trees are cut down each year to _____ _____ • it takes more energy to _____ _____ than plastic bags • only 12 percent of plastic bags are _____ _____

CONDENSE IDEAS

Paraphrase the first paragraph of Section 2 (*Issues,* p. 37–38). Keep important topic words and replace key words and phrases with synonyms.

Key Words & Phrases → Synonyms			
spokesperson	→ representative	Fido's	→ a pet's
defends	→ _____	plastics industry	→ makers of plastics
understand	→ grasp	encouraging	→ _____

Laurie Kusek, who represents the American Plastics Council, _____

_____

because the bags are _____

and she also says that makers of plastics _____

_____

IDENTIFY PRECISE WORDS

Review Section 2 and your *Portfolio* (pp. 86–87) to identify words for your argument.

Domain-Specific Topic Words	High-Utility Academic Words
• plastics industry	• implementation
•	•
•	•

Words to Go

 BUILD WORD KNOWLEDGE

Complete the meaning and examples for this high-utility academic word.

Word to Go	Meaning	Examples
occur oc•cur *verb*	to take place or _____	_____ does not **occur** often at our school. My favorite athletic event is the _____ _____ which **occurs** every _____

 DISCUSS & WRITE EXAMPLES

Discuss your response with a partner. Then complete the sentence in writing.

An example of a terrifying event that can **occur** without warning is (a/an) _____

_____

Write your response and read it aloud to a partner. Listen and record a new idea.

After the car accident _____ local police _____

_____

 BUILD WORD KNOWLEDGE

Complete the meaning and examples for this high-utility academic word.

Word to Go	Meaning	Examples
relevant rel•e•vant *adjective*	directly _____ to an issue or subject	The celebrity's message about _____ _____ is **relevant** to most teens' lives today. Yasmine found the article about girls and sports **relevant** because _____ _____

DISCUSS & WRITE EXAMPLES

Discuss your response with a partner. Then complete the sentence in writing.

The debate about whether to ban junk food is not **relevant** because our school

_____

Write your response and read it aloud to a partner. Listen and record a new idea.

During our discussion about whether graffiti should be considered art, I made a

_____ point that several cities now _____

Classmate's Name	Idea for *Occur*	Idea for *Relevant*

Close Reading

BUILD FLUENCY

Read Section 3 of "Ban It or Bag It?" (*Issues,* pp. 39–40).

IDENTIFY KEY IDEAS & DETAILS

Take turns asking and answering questions with a partner. Then write brief notes.

Discussion Frames	Text Notes
Q: What is the author's **main idea**? **A:** The author's **main idea** is _____ .	• most people agree that _____ _____
Q: What are the **key details** in this section? **A:** (One/Another) **key detail** in this section is _____ . **A:** Perhaps the **most important key detail** in this section is _____ .	• Americans may _____ because of the value they place on _____ • the Supreme Court of _____ said cities can _____ plastic bags • since then, more than _____ cities have banned bags

RESPOND WITH EVIDENCE

Use the frame and evidence from the text to construct a formal written response.

1. According to the author, why would a plastic bag ban be acceptable in China and India, but not in the United States?

According to the author, a ban against plastic bags may not be acceptable in the United States

because most Americans prefer to _____

_____

_____

Use the frame to analyze the author's word choice.

2. Why does the author use the word *staggering* on page 39 to describe the use of disposable plastic bags?

The author uses the word *staggering* to describe the use of disposable plastic bags because it

has a (positive/negative) _____ connotation. The word

staggering suggests that people use so many bags that it should _____

_____

IDENTIFY PRECISE WORDS

Review Section 3 and your *Portfolio* (pp. 88–89) to identify words for your argument.

Topic Words	High-Utility Words
• disposable • •	• occur • •

Academic Discussion
How can people use less plastic?

BRAINSTORM IDEAS

Briefly record at least two ideas in each column using everyday English.

At the Store	At Home
• carry a cloth bag • • •	• wear cotton, not polyester • • •

ANALYZE LANGUAGE

Complete the chart with precise words to discuss and write about the topic.

Everyday	Precise
use again *(verb)*	upcycle,
buying *(verb)*	acquiring,
things *(noun)*	products,

MAKE A CLAIM

Rewrite an idea using the frame and precise words. Then prepare to elaborate verbally.

Frame: One way people can use less plastic is by _____ (**verb + *–ing:*** encouraging, changing, reusing, choosing)

Response: _____

_____

_____

_____

_____

Language to ELABORATE
For instance, _____. The reason I know this is _____.

EXCHANGE IDEAS

Listen attentively, restate, and record your partner's idea.

Classmate's Name	Idea

Language to RESTATE
So your opinion is that _____. Yes, that's right. Actually, what I meant was _____.

Ten-Minute Response

A **ten-minute response** uses academic register. It begins with a well-stated **claim,** followed by **two detail sentences** that elaborate with relevant examples and precise words.

PRESENT IDEAS
Listen attentively and take notes. Then indicate if you agree (+) or disagree (–).

Language to AGREE/DISAGREE

I (agree/ disagree) with _____'s opinion.

Classmate's Name	Idea	+/–

Prompt	How can people use less plastic? Write a ten-minute response that states and supports your claim.

ELABORATE IN WRITING
Work with the teacher to write a ten-minute response in academic register.

Language to COLLABORATE

Let's think about what to write. A good option might be _____.

What are your thoughts? We could also try _____.

Okay. Let's write _____.

One way people can use less plastic is by preparing homemade cleaning products. For example, people can _____
a few simple ingredients and _____
As a result, people can _____
the number of plastic bottles they _____
_____

Work with a partner to write a ten-minute response in academic register.

One way people can use less plastic is by _____
_____

For example, you could choose to _____
_____

As a result, less plastic will end up in _____
_____

Words to Go

BUILD WORD KNOWLEDGE

Complete the meanings and examples for these high-utility academic words.

Words to Go	Meanings	Examples
potential po•ten•tial *noun*	the chance of something _____	The weatherman said tomorrow has a high **potential** for _____ _____
potential po•ten•tial *adjective*	a way of expressing _____	Alexi has studied the **potential** benefits of _____ _____

DISCUSS & WRITE EXAMPLES

Discuss your response with a partner. Then complete the sentence in writing.

According to today's sports report, there's a high **potential** for _____

_____

Write your response and read it aloud to a partner. Listen and record a new idea.

For a report last year, I researched the _____ causes of _____

_____

BUILD WORD KNOWLEDGE

Complete the meaning and examples for this high-utility academic word.

Word to Go	Meaning	Examples
ineffective in•ef•fec•tive *adjective*	not _____ at achieving the intended _____	My attempts to _____ _____ _____ were **ineffective**. _____ _____ is an **ineffective** way to study for a test.

DISCUSS & WRITE EXAMPLES

Discuss your response with a partner. Then complete the sentence in writing.

In my opinion, laws that restrict _____

_____ are **ineffective**.

Write your response and read it aloud to a partner. Listen and record a new idea.

The protest against animal testing was _____ and the company

continued to _____

Classmate's Name	Idea for *Potential*	Idea for *Ineffective*

Close Reading

BUILD FLUENCY

Read the text "With Millions of Tons of Plastic in Oceans, More Scientists Studying Impact" (*Issues*, pp. 41–44).

IDENTIFY KEY IDEAS & DETAILS

Take turns asking and answering questions with a partner. Then write brief notes.

Discussion Frames	Text Notes
Q: What is the author's **main idea**? **A:** The author's **main idea** is _____.	• the oceans have tons of _____ and _____

Q: What are the **key details** in this text?
 	
A: (One/Another) **key detail** in this text is _____.
 	
A: Perhaps the **most important key detail** in this text is _____.
	• cleaning up ocean debris is _____
	  _____
	
	• almost all ocean trash is _____
	  which is like a _____
	
	• all countries need to _____
	  so plastics don't end up in the ocean

RESPOND WITH EVIDENCE

Use the frame and evidence from the text to construct a formal written response.

1. According to the text, why is cleaning up garbage in the ocean challenging?

   Cleaning up the garbage in the ocean is challenging because it can also take away

   _____ which are important for the _____

   _____

   Cleaning up oceans is also a challenge because the trash is always _____

   _____

Use the frame to analyze the author's craft and structure.

2. What is the author's purpose? How does she convey that purpose?

   The author's purpose is to _____

   _____

   She conveys this purpose by including _____

   _____

IDENTIFY PRECISE WORDS

Review Text 2 and your *Portfolio* (pp. 90–93) to identify words for your argument.

Topic Words	High-Utility Words
• toxicity	• intervention
•	•
•	•

Analyze a Video

▶ **BUILD KNOWLEDGE**
Watch the video "Saving Our Synthetic Seas." Use the frames to discuss ideas with your group.

1. Something important I learned was _____.

2. I was particularly (fascinated/troubled) by _____.

✎ **LISTEN & TAKE NOTES**
Watch the video again. Listen closely and complete the outline.

I. Anna Cummins and Marcus Eriksen, the founders of the 5 Gyres Institute, created the "Saving Our Synthetic Seas" exhibit to _____

_____

II. The first item they describe is a _____ that they discovered with

_____ inside of it.

  A. The piece tells a story of _____

III. The second item in the exhibit, from "Junk Raft Adventure," is a _____

  for a boat made from _____

  _____

  A. The 5 Gyres Institute floated the boat from _____ to

  _____

  B. The piece shows the role of _____ in spreading _____

  _____

IV. A window display includes an albatross and tells the story of _____

  A. The bird's stomach contents include _____

  and _____

V. The exhibit also includes casts of _____

  A. The first cast is of Captain Charles Moore, who _____

  _____

  B. The second cast is of a young man, and it is made of _____

  C. The last cast is of Anna Cummins, and it is made of _____

  _____

VI. The final item in the exhibit is _____ the 5 Gyres Institute

  found between Tokyo and Hawaii, which shows that natural disasters leave _____

  _____ behind.

Language to COMPARE
What caught my attention was _____.
I particularly noted the fact that _____.
Like _____, I appreciated the way the (speaker/videographer) _____.

Close Viewing & Listening

Determining Central Ideas
To determine the **central idea** of a text, readers decide what is the most important overall idea, or message, the author wants to convey.

IDENTIFY KEY IDEAS & DETAILS
Use the frames to determine the central idea and analyze key details.

1. What is the central idea of the video?

   The central idea is that the 5 Gyres Institute has put together _____

   _____ to show how plastic pollution is

   _____

   _____

2. Why do you think one of the 5 Gyres Institute cofounders featured a real medical report next to the plastic cast of herself?

   Anna Cummins featured a real medical report next to the plastic cast of herself to show that

   plastics can _____

   The cast emphasizes this by _____

ANALYZE CRAFT & STRUCTURE
Use the frames to analyze the author's language choices.

3. One of the cofounders says the first piece in the exhibit "tells a story of entanglement." What is the effect of the word *entanglement*?

   The effect of one of the 5 Gyres cofounders saying the first piece tells "a story of

   entanglement" is that it shows how marine life in the ocean is trapped by the

   _____

   _____

   He uses the word *entanglement* to emphasize that the problem is _____

   _____

4. During the video, one of the cofounders says that single-use plastics can produce "mountains of trash" in the world's oceans. What is the effect of using the word *mountains*?

   The effect of Marcus Eriksen using *mountains* to describe ocean trash is that it shows that the

   amount of _____

   _____

   It helps viewers understand the size of the _____

Words to Go

 BUILD WORD KNOWLEDGE

Complete the meaning and examples for this high-utility academic word.

Word to Go	Meaning	Examples
generate gen•er•ate *verb*	to _____ or _____ something	Our team **generated** a lot of money when we _____ _____ The _____ _____ **generated** a huge amount of trash.

 DISCUSS & WRITE EXAMPLES

Discuss your response with a partner. Then complete the sentence in writing.

The student council hoped to **generate** several strong ideas about how to _____

_____

Write your response and read it aloud to a partner. Listen and record a new idea.

Hannah _____ a lot of interest when she arrived to school with a

new _____

 BUILD WORD KNOWLEDGE

Complete the meaning and examples for this high-utility academic word.

Word to Go	Meaning	Examples
alternative al•ter•na•tive *noun*	something you can choose _____ something else	I believe that _____ _____ is the best **alternative** to driving everywhere. The cafeteria offers a few **alternatives** for _____ _____

 DISCUSS & WRITE EXAMPLES

Discuss your response with a partner. Then complete the sentence in writing.

A useful **alternative** to _____

is _____

Write your response and read it aloud to a partner. Listen and record a new idea.

Hybrid and electric cars are great _____ to _____

Classmate's Name	Idea for *Generate*	Idea for *Alternative*

Close Reading

BUILD FLUENCY

Read "Bye-Bye Bags and Bottles: This Woman Lives Plastic Free" (*Issues,* pp. 45–47).

IDENTIFY KEY IDEAS & DETAILS

Take turns asking and answering questions with a partner. Then write brief notes.

Discussion Frames	Text Notes
Q: What is the author's **main idea**? **A:** The author's **main idea** is _____.	• Beth Terry decided to _____ _____
Q: What are the **key details** in this text? **A:** (One/Another) **key detail** in this text is _____. **A:** Perhaps the **most important key detail** in this text is _____.	• Terry lowered her plastic use to _____ _____ of the national average • she found _____ but still uses _____ • Terry's guidelines include storing food in _____ and making your own _____

RESPOND WITH EVIDENCE

Use the frame to analyze the author's word choice.

1. What is the meaning of the word *minimal* on page 46? What context clues helped you determine the meaning?

   The meaning of the word *minimal* is _____

   One context clue that helped me determine the meaning is that the text says Terry uses

   _____ and it lists two

   small _____

Use the frame to analyze the author's text structure.

2. Why did Kristine Wong include a list of Terry's guidelines for living plastic free?

   Wong included the list because she wanted to make the guidelines _____

   _____ so readers can _____

   _____

IDENTIFY PRECISE WORDS

Review Text 3 and your *Portfolio* (pp. 94–97) to identify words for your argument.

Domain-Specific Topic Words	High-Utility Academic Words
• zero-waste lifestyle • •	• deliberately • •

Student Writing Model

Academic Writing Type

An **argument** states a claim and supports it with logical reasons and relevant evidence from sources.

A. The **introduction** clearly states the writer's claim about the issue.

B. **Detail paragraphs** support the claim with reasons and evidence. The writer may also present counterclaims and respond with strong evidence.

C. The **conclusion** strongly restates the writer's claim about the issue.

D. **Transition words or phrases** connect ideas.

ANALYZE TEXT STRUCTURE

Read this student model to analyze the elements of an argument.

A

After examining the various issues surrounding a complete ban on disposable plastic bags, I contend that legislation prohibiting the distribution and use of disposable bags should not be instituted.

B1

A key reason I maintain this position is that consumers tend to use plastic bags responsibly. I've regularly witnessed individuals in my community, particularly in the park, reusing plastic bags to clean up after their pets or carry goods from place to place. In "Ban It or Bag It?," Sanjay Malik presents compelling data regarding the negative consequences of paper bags on the environment. For example, Malik describes how air and water pollution generated by the production of paper bags is greater than that caused by manufacturing plastic bags (38). On the other hand, proponents of an outright ban are likely to point out the fact that a higher percentage of paper bags than plastic bags is recycled. However, current data actually demonstrates that recycling paper bags uses more energy and plastic bags take up less space in landfills. (Malik 38).

B2

Another major reason I am opposed to limiting the use of plastic bags is because it restricts consumer freedom. As Oregon resident Judith McKenney states in "Ban It or Bag It?," using plastic bags is up to an individual to choose, not for a government to legislate. Similarly, one particularly interesting point that McKenney voices is that consumers can be responsible for their own bag use. This is important to consider because a way to be responsible, as Malik notes, is by paying taxes for the bags (37–39). Advocates for a total ban on plastic bag use may reply that these products last for up to 1,000 years in landfills despite the fact that some say a ban isn't relevant to what most Americans want (EcoWatch 35).

C

The controversial debate regarding whether cities should ban plastic bags will surely continue. However, after considering points on both sides of the issue and reviewing recent research, I strongly disapprove of government restrictions on plastic bags.

 MARK & DISCUSS ELEMENTS
Mark the argument elements and use the frames to discuss them with your partner.

1. **Put brackets around the writer's claim within the introduction.**
   The writer's claim is _____.

2. **Draw a box around four transition words or phrases.**
   One transition (word/phrase) is _____. Another transition (word/phrase) is _____.

3. **Underline and label two reasons that support the writer's claim with the letter _R_.**
   One reason that supports the writer's claim is _____.

4. **Underline and label four pieces of evidence that support the writer's claim with the letter _E_.**
   One reason that supports the writer's claim is _____.

5. **Double underline two counterclaims.**
   One counterclaim is _____. The writer responds by _____.

6. **Star four precise topic words and check four high-utility academic words.**
   An example of a (precise topic word/high-utility academic word) is _____.

Precise Adjectives for Evidence

Guidelines for Using Precise Adjectives for Evidence
Use **precise adjectives** to describe the data, statistics, and other evidence you present to support your claim.

Everyday Adjectives	Precise Adjectives
good	convincing, powerful, strong, compelling, relevant
scary	alarming, distressing, unnerving, striking, disturbing
hard	difficult, troubling, challenging, complex, complicated
new	recent, current, up-to-date
enough/true-sounding	sufficient, adequate, substantial, believable, convincing
silly	absurd, preposterous, ridiculous, unreasonable
not enough/untrue	insufficient, unfounded, baseless, unsubstantiated

WRITE PRECISE ADJECTIVES
Complete the sentences with precise adjectives.

1. (A/An) _____ statistic about video games is that almost 10 percent of gamers are addicted.

2. One particularly _____ statistic cited in the article is that neighborhoods with graffiti sometimes experience more crime.

3. After considering points on both sides of the issue and reviewing _____ research, I strongly support a ban on vending machines in school.

Use precise adjectives to complete the sentences about the claim.

Claim: Video games benefit teens.

1. Evidence: In "Game On or Game Over?," Oscar Gomez presents _____ data regarding the positive consequences of playing video games.

2. Evidence: One particularly _____ statistic is that 65 percent of teen gamers play along with other people in the same room.

3. Counterclaim: Although a common argument against video games is that gamers do poorly in school, I don't find the evidence _____

4. Response to Counterclaim: However, _____ evidence actually demonstrates that video games can improve performance in certain areas.

5. Restating Claim: After considering points on both sides of the issue and reviewing _____ research, I strongly disagree that video games are unhealthy for teens.

Modal & Conditional Verbs

Guidelines for Using Modal & Conditional Verbs

Modal and **conditional verbs** describe what is possible or preferable. They show what conditions would be like if a recommendation became reality.

Will, shall, may (+ base verb) show a real future possibility:

*A tax on plastic bags **may reduce** the amount of bags used by consumers.*

Would, should, could, might (+ base verb) show an uncertain future possibility:

*If more people use alternatives to plastic, our air quality **could improve**.*

Would have, should have, could have, might have (+ past participle) show a past impossibility:

*When researchers discovered garbage patches, officials **should have passed** legislation to address the issue.*

 IDENTIFY VERBS

Read the argument paragraphs and circle the modal and conditional verbs.

A key reason I maintain this position is that making it easy for consumers to recycle plastic bags will decrease the number of bags that end up in landfills. In "Ban It or Bag It?," Sanjay Malik presents compelling data regarding the negative consequences of producing plastic bags. For example, the bags that people throw away today could last more than 1,000 years. Opponents of a plastic bag ban tend to highlight that consumers should recycle the bags. However, current data actually demonstrate that less than five percent of people recycle bags.

Another major reason I support legislation is because it would reduce pollution. The Shaping Environmental Education Knowledge website emphasizes that plastic bags clog drainage lines. One particularly convincing statistic is that bags caused two-thirds of Bangladesh to be submerged after floods in 1998. The country could have avoided that if it had a recycling plan.

 USE VERBS CORRECTLY

Use a modal or conditional verb to complete each sentence.

1. Implementing a ban on plastic bags _____

2. If every state had imposed a tax on plastic bags in 2010, when Washington, DC, did,

fewer bags _____

3. Proponents of a plastic bag ban claim that it _____

_____

4. Making plastic bags easier to recycle _____

_____

Organize an Argument

Prompt Should cities outlaw plastic bags? Write an argument that states your claim and supports it with text evidence.

Transitions to Create Cohesion	Examples
Similarly, _____. Just as, _____. In the same way, _____. However, _____. On the other hand, _____. Although _____, _____. Despite _____, _____.	**Just as** car emissions pollute the air, microplastics pollute the oceans. **Although** plastic bag manufacturers claim bags are recyclable, very few are ultimately recycled. **On the other hand,** 15 to 20 percent of paper bags are recycled.

IDENTIFY TRANSITIONS

Review the transitions that writers use to create cohesion. Then complete each sentence below with an appropriate transition.

1. _____ the gyres Cummins sampled both showed evidence of plastic pollution.

2. _____ cleaning beaches can help somewhat, solving the problem of garbage patches will require more effort.

3. _____ no matter where the garbage originates, it may end up in the oceans.

WRITE AN INTRODUCTION
State your claim.

My claim: _____

Use academic language to restate your claim in an introduction.

After examining the various issues surrounding _____
(topic)

I _____ that _____
(verb to express opinion) (claim)

_____

CHOOSE SUPPORTING TOPICS
List each topic you will write about to support your claim.

Supporting Paragraph 1

Topic: _____

_____

Supporting Paragraph 2

Topic: _____

_____

PLAN SUPPORTING PARAGRAPHS
List reasons and evidence that support your claim.

Supporting Paragraph 1

Reason 1: _____

_____

Evidence: _____

_____

Source/Page Number: _____

Author: _____

Counterclaim: _____

_____

Response to Counterclaim: _____

_____

Source: _____

Author: _____

Supporting Paragraph 2

Reason 2: _____

_____

Evidence: _____

_____

Source/Page Number: _____

_____

Author: _____

Statistical Evidence: _____

_____

Source/Page Number: _____

WRITE A CONCLUSION
Plan a conclusion that restates your claim.

The controversial debate regarding _____
                                    (restate the issue)

_____ will surely continue.

However, after considering points on both sides of the issue and

reviewing _____ research, I strongly (approve/disapprove)
          (adjective: recent, relevant, substantial)

_____ of _____ plastic bags.
                              (noun phrase: bans on, laws opposing, government restrictions on)

Write an Argument

Prompt   Should cities outlaw plastic bags? Write an argument that states your claim and supports it with text evidence.

✎ WRITE AN ESSAY

Use the frame to write your introduction, detail paragraphs, and conclusion.

A

After examining the _____ issues surrounding
(adjective: various, numerous, multiple)

a complete ban on _____ bags, I _____
(adjective: plastic, single-use)   (verb phrase to express opinion)

that legislation prohibiting the distribution and use of disposable bags

(should/should not) _____ be _____
(past participle: passed, enacted, instituted)

B1

A key reason I maintain this position is that consumers tend to

_____ plastic bags _____
(base verb: utilize, use, employ)   (adverb: responsibly, thoughtfully, irresponsibly, recklessly)

I have regularly _____ individuals in my community,
(past-tense verb: observed, noticed, witnessed)

particularly _____
(location: at school, in my apartment complex, on the street, in the park)

_____   _____
(verb + –ing: wasting, littering, reusing, recycling)   (evidence from your experience)

_____

_____

_____

In _____
(title of source)

_____ presents _____
(author's full name)   (adjective)

data regarding the (negative/positive) _____ consequences

of _____ consumers to _____
(verb + –ing: relying on, expecting, permitting)   (base verb: recycle, reuse, conserve, carry)

_____

_____

For example, _____ describes how _____
(author's last name)   (evidence from text)

_____

_____

_____

B1

On the other hand, (opponents/proponents) _____ of an

outright ban are likely to _____ the fact that this extreme

(base verb: point out, highlight, emphasize)

measure would _____ _____

(base verb: allow, encourage, force, reduce)   (evidence from text)

_____

_____

_____

_____

However, _____

(adjective + plural noun: current data, recent research, well-known facts)

actually demonstrate that _____

(evidence from text)

_____

_____

_____

_____

B2

Another major reason I am (in favor of/opposed to) _____

_____ the use of plastic bags is the fact that

(verb + -ing: restricting, controlling, outlawing)

pollution caused by plastic bag debris _____

(present-tense verb: endangers, damages, harms, pollutes)

_____

_____

_____

_____

_____ emphasizes

(author's name)

in _____

(title of source)

the _____ impacts of plastic on the environment.

(adjective)

B2

_____ one particularly
(transition to create cohesion)

_____ statistic cited by _____ is that
(adjective)   (author's last name)

_____
(evidence from text)

_____

_____

This is important to consider because _____
                                                     (evidence from text or your experience)

_____

_____

_____

_____

(Critics/Advocates) _____ of a _____
                                                          (adjective: complete, comprehensive, total)

ban on plastic bag use may reply that these products are

_____ despite the fact that _____
(adjective: necessary, wasteful, convenient)   (evidence from text)

_____

_____

_____

_____

C

The controversial debate regarding _____
                                                     (restate the issue)

_____

_____ will surely continue.

However, after considering _____ on both sides
                                          (plural noun: points of view, perspectives, arguments)

of the issue and reviewing _____ research, I strongly
                                         (adjective)

(approve/disapprove) _____ of legislation that would

_____ the use of plastic bags.
(base verb: outlaw, ban, prohibit)

Rate Your Argument

ASSESS YOUR DRAFT
Rate your argument. Then have a partner rate it.

Scoring Guide
① Insufficient
② Developing
③ Sufficient
④ Exemplary

1. Does the introduction clearly state your claim?	Self	①	②	③	④
	Partner	①	②	③	④
2. Did you include strong reasons and text evidence to support your claim?	Self	①	②	③	④
	Partner	①	②	③	④
3. Did you include a counterclaim and respond with strong evidence?	Self	①	②	③	④
	Partner	①	②	③	④
4. Did you include citation information for evidence from texts?	Self	①	②	③	④
	Partner	①	②	③	④
5. Did you use transitions to introduce reasons and evidence?	Self	①	②	③	④
	Partner	①	②	③	④
6. Did you include precise topic words and high-utility academic words?	Self	①	②	③	④
	Partner	①	②	③	④
7. Does the conclusion strongly restate the claim?	Self	①	②	③	④
	Partner	①	②	③	④

REFLECT & REVISE
Record specific priorities and suggestions to help you and your partner revise.

(Partner) Positive Feedback: You did an effective job of (using/including/explaining)

_____

_____

(Partner) Suggestion: Your argument will be stronger if you (include/improve/explain)

_____

_____

(Self) Priority 1: I will revise my argument so that it (includes/develops/explains)

_____

_____

(Self) Priority 2: I also need to (add/revise/check) _____

_____

CHECK & EDIT
Use this checklist to proofread and edit your argument.

☐ Did you format citations correctly?

☐ Did you use commas appropriately after transitions?

☐ Did you use verb tenses appropriately?

☐ Is each sentence complete?

☐ Are all words spelled correctly?

Informative Speech

Prompt How does plastic debris affect oceans? Present a speech that provides important details to develop the topic.

BRAINSTORM IDEAS
Write a topic sentence that states the main idea.

Topic sentence: Plastic debris affects oceans by _____

_____

_____

IDENTIFY EVIDENCE
Take notes on evidence from the text or your experience that supports your claim.

Supporting Detail 1: _____

_____

_____

Supporting Detail 2: _____

_____

_____

WRITE A SPEECH
With a partner, write a speech that develops your topic. Use visuals or multimedia to clarify information and add interest.

Plastic affects the oceans by (threatening/poisoning/polluting) _____

_____

One (fact/example) _____ that supports this idea is that _____

_____

_____

Similarly, plastic debris has also affected the _____

_____

_____

Perhaps the largest effect plastic debris has on the oceans is how _____

_____

_____

These reasons lead many people to believe that plastic debris affects the oceans in ways

that are _____

_____

_____

Present & Rate Your Speech

Using Adequate Volume

When presenting ideas during class, use **adequate volume**. Speak three times louder than your everyday voice. People who are farther away need to hear you, and you want them to understand you the first time.

PRESENT YOUR SPEECH
Present your speech to the small group. Make sure to use adequate volume.

LISTEN & TAKE NOTES
Listen attentively and take notes.
Then indicate if you agree (+) or disagree (–).

Language to AFFIRM & CLARIFY

I heard you say _____. However, _____.
What do you mean by _____?

Classmate's Name	Idea	+/–

ASSESS YOUR SPEECH
Use the Scoring Guide to rate your speech.

Scoring Guide

① Insufficient	③ Sufficient
② Developing	④ Exemplary

1. Did you develop a topic with definitions, relevant facts, and concrete details?	① ② ③ ④
2. Did you use precise topic words?	① ② ③ ④
3. Did you provide a strong conclusion?	① ② ③ ④
4. Did you use adequate volume?	① ② ③ ④
5. Did you include visual displays or multimedia to clarify information?	① ② ③ ④

REFLECT
Write two ways you can improve your next speech.

Priority 1: I can strengthen my next speech by (including/changing) _____

_____

_____

Priority 2: In my next speech, I will incorporate _____

_____

_____

Issue 5 Texting

LEARNING & LANGUAGE GOALS
Check your learning in this Issue against the objectives on pages 6–7.

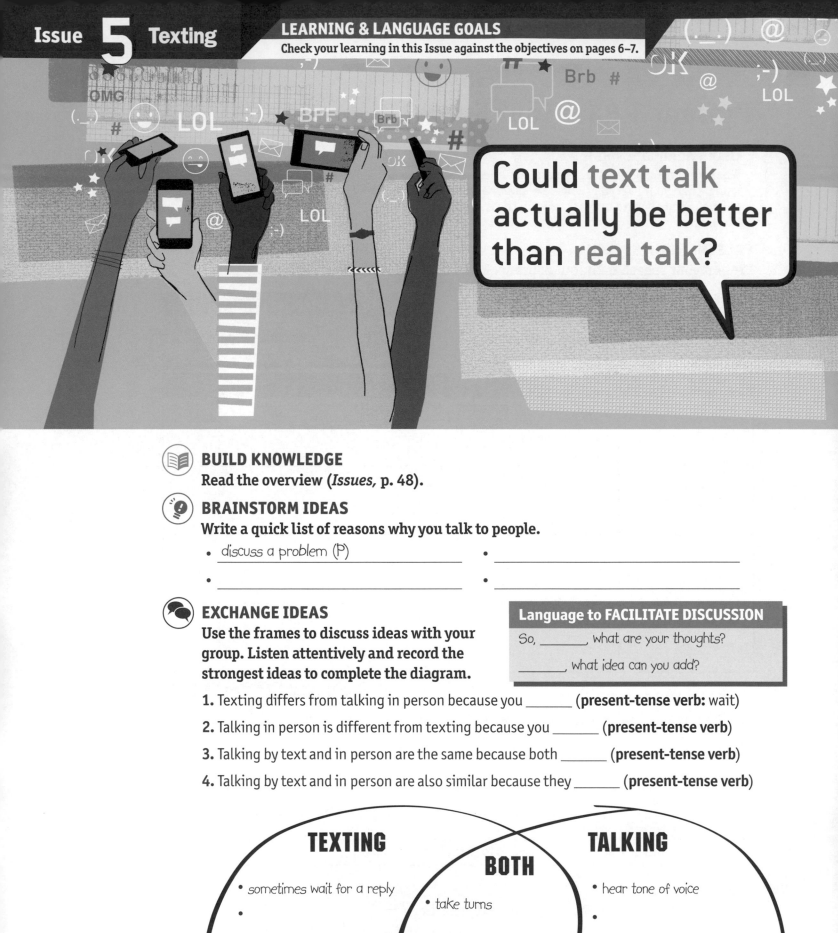

Could text talk actually be better than real talk?

BUILD KNOWLEDGE
Read the overview (*Issues*, p. 48).

BRAINSTORM IDEAS
Write a quick list of reasons why you talk to people.

- discuss a problem (P)
- _____
- _____
- _____

EXCHANGE IDEAS
Use the frames to discuss ideas with your group. Listen attentively and record the strongest ideas to complete the diagram.

Language to FACILITATE DISCUSSION
So, _____, what are your thoughts?
_____, what idea can you add?

1. Texting differs from talking in person because you _____ (**present-tense verb:** wait)

2. Talking in person is different from texting because you _____ (**present-tense verb**)

3. Talking by text and in person are the same because both _____ (**present-tense verb**)

4. Talking by text and in person are also similar because they _____ (**present-tense verb**)

TEXTING
- sometimes wait for a reply
- •
- •

BOTH
- take turns
- •
- •

TALKING
- hear tone of voice
- •
- •

Words to Know

Language to COMPARE
Our example builds
upon _____'s group's.

BUILD WORD KNOWLEDGE

Rate your word knowledge. Then discuss word meanings and examples with your group.

		① Don't Know	② Recognize	③ Familiar	④ Know

Words to Know	Meanings	Examples
1 distract *verb* ① ② ③ ④	to take someone's _____ away from what he or she is doing	I tried to **distract** my brother so that he wouldn't notice that I was _____ _____ I don't like to do my homework _____ _____ because the noise **distracts** me.
2 formal *adjective* ① ② ③ ④	official; not _____	I would never wear _____ _____ to a **formal** event I made sure to use **formal** language when I _____ _____
3 technical *adjective* ① ② ③ ④	related to _____ science, or _____	My **technical** abilities include being able to _____ _____ When my _____ stopped working, I needed **technical** support.
4 technology *noun* ① ② ③ ④	the use of science and _____	My grandfather is unwilling to embrace new **technologies**, so he still uses _____ _____ _____ Cell phone **technology** makes _____ _____ _____ much easier.

Language to FACILITATE DISCUSSION

I've never seen or heard the word _____.

I recognize the word _____ but need to learn how to use it.

I can use _____ in a sentence. For example, _____.

I know that the word _____ means _____.

We are unfamiliar with the word _____.

We recognize the word _____, but we would benefit from a review of what it means and how to use it.

We think _____ means _____.

Building Concepts

DEVELOP UNDERSTANDING
Complete the organizer to build your knowledge of the concept.

communicate *(verb)*

Example Sentence

As long as we can **communicate** our thoughts and feelings with others effectively, does it really matter whether we're **communicating** with spoken words, gestures, or texts?

Synonyms	Word Family
Everyday: Precise: • _____ • _____ • _____ • _____	• communicate *(verb)* • communication *(noun)* • communicative *(adjective)*

Meaning	Essential Characteristics

to _____
 	
 information or _____
 	
 with others
	• sending a _____
	   that someone else _____
	 • building _____
	   and _____ between people

Examples	Non-Examples
• writing a letter • _____ _____ _____ • _____ _____ _____	• not answering a call • _____ _____ _____ • _____ _____ _____

Write About It

Many young people **communicate** with their friends by _____

_____

and _____

As a result, their **communication** tends to be _____

BUILD KNOWLEDGE
Read and respond to the Data File (*Issues,* p. 49). Use the frames to discuss ideas with your group.

1. One finding that caught my attention is _____ because _____.

2. One statistic that didn't surprise me at all is _____ because _____.

Language to FACILITATE DISCUSSION

I am eager to hear from _____.

I nominate _____.

Words to Know

BUILD WORD KNOWLEDGE

Rate your word knowledge. Then discuss word meanings and examples with your group.

Language to COMPARE

Our example builds
upon _____'s group's.

	① Don't Know	② Recognize	③ Familiar	④ Know

Words to Know	Meanings	Examples
1 bond *noun* ①②③④	a close _____ with or strong _____ for someone	When I was little, I had a special **bond** with my _____ The **bonds** between _____ and their _____ can be intense.
2 code *noun* ①②③④	a set of _____ that tell people how to _____	_____ violates the dress **code** at some schools. _____ is against the school's honor **code**.
3 norm *noun* ①②③④	an agreed-upon way of behaving _____	In the cafeteria, social **norms** influence _____ I saw a movie about a girl who went against the **norms** of her social group by _____
4 proper *adjective* ①②③④	_____ or appropriate for a situation	An example of **proper** dress for a job interview in an office is _____ A **proper** way to respond when you aren't sure you understood someone is to say, _____

Language to FACILITATE DISCUSSION

I've never seen or heard the word _____.

I recognize the word _____ but need to learn how to use it.

I can use _____ in a sentence. For example, _____.

I know that the word _____ means _____.

We are unfamiliar with the word _____.

We recognize the word _____, but we would benefit from a review of what it means and how to use it.

We think _____ means _____.

Academic Discussion

How is texting changing the way we communicate?

BRAINSTORM IDEAS

Briefly record at least two ideas in each column using everyday English.

In Writing	In Person
• teens are writing more because they text everyday	• making us less patient
•	•
•	•
•	•

ANALYZE LANGUAGE

Complete the chart with precise words to discuss and write about the topic.

Everyday	Precise
feel bad about *(verb)*	rue,
say *(verb)*	articulate,
nice *(adjective)*	civil,

MAKE A CLAIM

Rewrite an idea using the frame and precise words. Then prepare to elaborate verbally.

Frame: Texting is changing the way we communicate by making us (more/less) likely to _____ (**base verb:** use, rely on, write, communicate)

Response: _____

_____

_____

_____

Language to ELABORATE

For example, _____.

This is the case because _____.

EXCHANGE IDEAS

Listen attentively, restate, and record your partner's idea.

Classmate's Name	Idea

Language to RESTATE

So your perspective is that _____.

Yes, that's correct.

No, not exactly. What I meant was _____.

Ten-Minute Response

A **ten-minute response** uses academic register. It begins with a well-stated **claim,** followed by **two detail sentences** that elaborate with relevant examples and precise words.

PRESENT IDEAS
Listen attentively and take notes. Then write if you agree (+) or disagree (–).

Language to AGREE/DISAGREE

I completely (agree/disagree) with _____'s perspective.

Classmate's Name	Idea	+/–

Prompt	How is texting changing the way we communicate? Write a ten-minute response that states and supports your claim.

ELABORATE IN WRITING
Work with the teacher to write a ten-minute response in academic register.

Language to COLLABORATE

What should we write? We could try _____.

Do you agree? Another option is _____.

Okay. Let's write _____.

Texting is changing the way we communicate by making us less likely to follow social norms regarding greetings. For example, when meeting in person, most teens will greet friends by _____

_____

but when texting, they usually _____

_____

As a result, texting tends to be _____
but it is also _____

Write a ten-minute response on your own using academic register.

Texting is changing the way we communicate by making us _____

likely to _____

For example, when texting, I can include _____

_____ to tell my friends

that I _____

_____

As a result, we appreciate _____

_____

Words to Go

 BUILD WORD KNOWLEDGE

Complete the meanings and examples for these high-utility academic words.

Words to Go	Meanings	Examples
connect con•nect *verb*	to _____ one thing with another	At _____ _____ I **connected** with new friends.
connection con•nec•tion *noun*	a _____ between objects, people, or ideas	Ezra's strong **connection** with his _____ won't be broken when he _____ _____

 DISCUSS & WRITE EXAMPLES

Discuss your response with a partner. Then complete the sentence in writing.

When we **connect** with _____ those relationships

can help us through _____

Write your response and read it aloud to a partner. Listen and record a new idea.

Marcus felt an immediate _____ to the book's main character because

both of them have _____

BUILD WORD KNOWLEDGE

Complete the meaning and examples for this high-utility academic word.

Word to Go	Meaning	Examples
constant con•stant *adjective*	happening _____ _____	In my life, _____ (is/are) a **constant** source of help. Once the school year gets going, there is a **constant** stream of _____ _____

DISCUSS & WRITE EXAMPLES

Discuss your response with a partner. Then complete the sentence in writing.

Professional athletes aim for **constant** improvement when it comes to _____

_____

Write your response and read it aloud to a partner. Listen and record a new idea.

_____

_____ is a _____ concern in my life.

Classmate's Name	Idea for *Connect/Connection*	Idea for *Constant*

Section Shrink

BUILD FLUENCY

Read Section 1 of "luv 2 txt" (*Issues,* pp. 50–51).

IDENTIFY KEY IDEAS & DETAILS

Take turns asking and answering questions with a partner. Then write brief notes.

Discussion Frames	Text Notes
Q: What is this section **primarily about**? **A:** This section is **primarily about** _____.	• how texting is a _____ way for teens to _____

Q: What are the **most essential details** in this section?
 	
A: (One/An additional) **essential detail** in this section is _____.
 	
A: Perhaps the **most essential** detail in this section is _____.
	• _____ of American
	
	   teens who use cell phones send more than
	
	   _____ texts each day
	• many _____
	
	   worry that too much texting
	
	   is _____
	• experts like Professor Larry Rosen say having
	
	   more _____
	
	   is _____

CONDENSE IDEAS

Paraphrase Section 1 of the text by combining key information into one sentence. Replace key words and phrases with synonyms and keep important topic words.

Key Words & Phrases → Synonyms			
one-third	→ many	harmful	→ detrimental
send	→ _____	more connections	→ _____
daily	→ _____	good	→ beneficial

Many teens _____

hundreds of texts every day, and the distractions might be _____

but the _____

might be _____

IDENTIFY PRECISE WORDS

Review Section 1 and your *Portfolio* (pp. 110–117) to identify words for your writing.

Domain-Specific Topic Words	High-Utility Academic Words
• distracting	• communicate
•	•
•	•

Words to Go

Language to LISTEN ACTIVELY

What example did you appreciate? I appreciated _____.

What example did you relate to? I related to _____.

 BUILD WORD KNOWLEDGE

Complete the meaning and examples for this high-utility academic word.

Word to Go	Meaning	Examples
admit ad•mit *verb*	to _____ or announce information as _____	After staying up too late, I **admitted** to feeling _____ the next day. I didn't want to **admit** to my friend that I don't like his _____

 DISCUSS & WRITE EXAMPLES

Discuss your response with a partner. Then complete the sentence in writing.

I don't mind **admitting** that I can sometimes be _____

_____

Write your response and read it aloud to a partner. Listen and record a new idea.

After we finished the group project, my classmate _____

that she could have _____

 BUILD WORD KNOWLEDGE

Complete the meanings and examples for these high-utility academic words.

Words to Go	Meanings	Examples
constructive con•struc•tive *adjective*	_____ for improvement on a project or issue	I appreciate **constructive** criticism about how I can do a better job of _____ _____
constructively con•struc•tive•ly *adverb*	in a way that is _____ and _____	After school, I am going to use my time **constructively** to _____ _____

 DISCUSS & WRITE EXAMPLES

Discuss your response with a partner. Then complete the sentence in writing.

When we work in groups, our teacher gives us suggestions for how to be **constructive**

when we _____

Write your response and read it aloud to a partner.

I think our school should have workshops about how to deal _____

with _____

Classmate's Name	Idea for *Admit*	Idea for *Constructive/Constructively*

Section Shrink

 BUILD FLUENCY
Read Section 2 of "luv 2 txt" (*Issues,* p. 51).

 IDENTIFY KEY IDEAS & DETAILS
Take turns asking and answering questions with a partner. Then write brief notes.

Discussion Frames	Text Notes
Q: What is this section **primarily about**? **A:** This section is **primarily about** _____.	• the _____ of texting
Q: What are the **most essential details** in this section? **A:** (One/An additional) **essential detail** in this section is _____. **A:** Perhaps the most **essential** detail in this section is _____.	• texting can improve teens' _____, _____, and _____ skills • texting is the _____ form of _____ for teens • Professor Scott Campbell believes texting _____ _____ between teens

 CONDENSE IDEAS
Paraphrase Section 2 of the text by combining key information into one sentence. Replace key words and phrases with synonyms and keep important topic words.

Key Words & Phrases → Synonyms			
improve	→ increase		
skills	→ _____	strengthening	→ _____
doing something else	→ multitasking	social bonds	→ _____

Texting can benefit teens by _____ their

language _____, allowing them to multitask,

and _____ their _____.

IDENTIFY PRECISE WORDS
Review Section 2 and your *Portfolio* (pp. 118–119) to identify words for your writing.

Domain-Specific Topic Words	High-Utility Academic Words
• interacting • •	• improve • •

Words to Go

Language to LISTEN ACTIVELY

What example did you appreciate? I appreciated _____.

What example did you relate to? I related to _____.

BUILD WORD KNOWLEDGE

Complete the meaning and examples for this high-utility academic word.

Word to Go	Meaning	Examples
affect af•fect *verb*	to _____ someone or something	_____ **affects** what I decide to wear in the morning. _____ _____ would positively **affect** my grades.

DISCUSS & WRITE EXAMPLES

Discuss your response with a partner. Then complete the sentence in writing.

The _____

of a cell phone would **affect** my decision about whether to buy it.

Write your response and read it aloud to a partner. Listen and record a new idea.

Some students think that _____

will _____ their popularity.

BUILD WORD KNOWLEDGE

Complete the meaning and examples for this high-utility academic word.

Word to Go	Meaning	Examples
demonstrate dem•on•strate *verb*	to _____ a particular ability, quality, or feeling	Young children often **demonstrate** their hunger by _____ _____ My aunt said that I **demonstrated** responsibility when I _____ _____ without being reminded.

DISCUSS & WRITE EXAMPLES

Discuss your response with a partner. Then complete the sentence in writing.

Students who **demonstrate** an interest in _____

should consider _____

Write your response and read it aloud to a partner. Listen and record a new idea.

In last year's school play, Monica _____ a talent for _____

_____

Classmate's Name	Idea for *Affect*	Idea for *Demonstrate*

Close Reading

BUILD FLUENCY

Read Section 3 of "luv 2 txt" (*Issues,* pp. 52–53).

IDENTIFY KEY IDEAS & DETAILS

Take turns asking and answering questions with a partner. Then write brief notes.

Discussion Frames	Text Notes
Q: What is this section **primarily about**? **A:** This section is **primarily about** _____.	• the _____ and _____ of texting
Q: What are the **most essential details** in this section? **A:** (One/An additional) **essential detail** in this section is _____. **A:** Perhaps the **most essential** detail in this section is _____.	• technology is helping teens make more _____ • some teachers worry that texting has a negative influence on _____ _____ • a study shows that teens who use _____ have better _____ skills • 15-year-old Jenny Kreps says texting makes her more _____

RESPOND WITH EVIDENCE

Use the frame and evidence from the text to construct a formal written response.

1. According to the text, what does texting provide for teens?

According to the text, texting gives teens _____

It follows different _____ such as using _____

_____

Use the frame to analyze the author's word choice.

2. What is the meaning of the word *competent* on page 53? What context clue helped you determine the meaning?

The meaning of the word *competent* is _____

One context clue that helped me determine the meaning is that _____

_____

IDENTIFY PRECISE WORDS

Review Section 3 and your *Portfolio* (pp. 120–121) to identify words for your writing.

Domain-Specific Topic Words	High-Utility Academic Words
• *sociable* • •	• *peers* • •

Academic Discussion

Does texting tend to hurt writing skills?

BRAINSTORM IDEAS

Briefly record at least two ideas in each column using everyday English.

Agree	Disagree
• use textisms instead of words	• write faster
•	•
•	•
•	•

ANALYZE LANGUAGE

Complete the chart with precise words to discuss and write about the topic.

Everyday	Precise
go from one to another *(verb)*	code switch,
have to have *(verb)*	depend on,
easily *(adverb)*	effortlessly,

MAKE A CLAIM

Rewrite an idea using the frame and precise words. Then prepare to elaborate verbally.

Frame: From my point of view, texting (does/does not) tend to hurt writing skills because people _____ (**present-tense verb:** express, use, shift, communicate)

Response: _____

_____

_____

_____

Language to ELABORATE

For example, _____.

This is the case because _____.

EXCHANGE IDEAS

Listen attentively, restate, and record your partner's idea.

Classmate's Name	Idea

Language to RESTATE

So your perspective is that _____.

Yes, that's correct.

No, not exactly. What I meant was _____.

Ten-Minute Response

A **ten-minute response** uses academic register. It begins with a well-stated **claim,** followed by **two detail sentences** that elaborate with relevant examples and precise words.

PRESENT IDEAS
Listen attentively and take notes. Then indicate if you agree (+) or disagree (–).

Language to AGREE/DISAGREE

I completely (agree/disagree) with _____'s perspective.

Classmate's Name	Idea	+/–

Prompt	Does texting tend to hurt writing skills? Write a ten-minute response that states and supports your claim.

ELABORATE IN WRITING
Work with the teacher to write a ten-minute response in academic register.

Language to COLLABORATE

What should we write? We could try _____.

Do you agree? Another option is _____.

Okay. Let's write _____.

From my point of view, texting does tend to hurt writing skills because people rely on shortcuts too frequently. For example, with texting, you can _____

_____

rather than _____

As a result, when people who text frequently need to use more formal writing to express themselves, they might _____

_____

Write a ten-minute response on your own using academic register.

From my point of view, texting _____ tend to hurt writing skills because people _____

_____

For example, when texting, I may need to _____

_____

_____

As a result, I _____

_____

_____

Words to Go

Language to LISTEN ACTIVELY

What example did you appreciate? I appreciated _____.

What example did you relate to? I related to _____.

BUILD WORD KNOWLEDGE

Complete the meanings and examples for these high-utility academic words.

Words to Go	Meanings	Examples
convenience con•ven•ience *noun*	something that makes a person's life _____	I enjoy the **convenience** of living close to _____ _____
convenient con•ven•ient *adjective*	_____ to have or access	Even though going to the party wasn't very **convenient**, I went because I _____ _____

DISCUSS & WRITE EXAMPLES

Discuss your response with a partner. Then complete the sentence in writing.

The Internet is an incredible **convenience** for _____

_____

Write your response and read it aloud to a partner. Listen and record a new idea.

Eating _____

is _____ but not the healthiest choice.

BUILD WORD KNOWLEDGE

Complete the meaning and examples for this high-utility academic word.

Word to Go	Meaning	Examples
decline de•cline *noun*	a _____ in the quality, quantity, or importance of something	To reverse the **decline** in my grades, I need to _____ Since I _____ _____ I've had a **decline** in my free time.

DISCUSS & WRITE EXAMPLES

Discuss your response with a partner. Then complete the sentence in writing.

A new school program has led to a sharp **decline** in _____

_____

Write your response and read it aloud to a partner. Listen and record a new idea.

To encourage a _____ in car accidents, the city has _____

_____

Classmate's Name	Idea for *Convenience/Convenient*	Idea for *Decline*

Close Reading

BUILD FLUENCY

Read the text "LOL, Texting, and Txt-speak: Linguistic Miracles" (*Issues,* pp. 54–56).

IDENTIFY KEY IDEAS & DETAILS

Take turns asking and answering questions with a partner. Then write brief notes.

Discussion Frames	Text Notes
Q: What is this text **primarily about**? **A:** This text is **primarily about** _____.	• how texting is a new _____ _____
Q: What are the **most essential details** in this text? **A:** (One/An additional) **essential detail** in this text is _____. **A:** Perhaps the **most essential detail** in this text is _____.	• people have been speaking for at least _____ but only writing for about _____ • Linguist John McWhorter says texting allows us to _____ • texting is like speaking because it often leaves out _____ and _____

RESPOND WITH EVIDENCE

Use the frame and evidence from the text to construct a formal written response.

1. According to the blog post, how is texting "a whole new language"?

According to the blog post, texting is " a whole new language" because it is _____

_____

It is also creating new language conventions, such as "LOL," which can mean _____

_____

or just _____

Use the frame to evaluate the author's evidence.

2. What evidence supports John McWhorter's idea that texting is not "really writing"?

Evidence to support McWhorter's idea that texting is not "really writing" includes the

example that we speak using _____

He also points out that texting often ignores _____

_____

IDENTIFY PRECISE WORDS

Review Text 2 and your *Portfolio* (pp. 122–125) to identify words for your writing.

Domain-Specific Topic Words	High-Utility Academic Words
• texting shorthand	• convenience
•	•
•	•

Analyze a Podcast

▶ **BUILD KNOWLEDGE**

Listen to the podcast "Crisis Texting With Bob Filbin." Use the frames to discuss ideas with your partner.

1. Something that surprised me was _____.

2. I noticed that the interviewer _____.

✏ **LISTEN & TAKE NOTES**

Listen closely to the podcast again. Complete the outline.

I. Originally, the organization DoSomething.org sent teens texts about _____

_____

    A. Sometimes, teens texted back about unrelated topics, such as _____

    _____ or _____

    B. CEO Nancy Lublin founded Crisis Text Line in 2013 because she realized that teens needed

    a _____

    _____

II. Bob Filbin, the chief data scientist at Crisis Text Line, analyzes data from the service.

    A. He found that teens want someone who will _____

    _____

    B. Filbin improves efficiency by collecting information about how to improve the

    software that volunteers use to _____

    C. In the first six months of the service, counselors and teens exchanged more than

    _____ messages.

III. Identifying patterns helps Crisis Text Line support teens.

    A. Some of the busiest times are _____

    and _____

    B. Teens reach out about _____

    on _____

IV. Because texting is a unique _____

it has benefits for crisis support.

    A. Texting is _____ so teens can get help while they are

    _____

    B. Texting is also _____ and _____

Language to COMPARE
What caught my attention was _____.
I particularly noted the fact that _____.
Like _____, I appreciated the way the speaker _____.

Close Listening

IDENTIFY KEY IDEAS & DETAILS
Use the frames to analyze key details and make inferences.

1. How is Crisis Text Line helping teens?

One way Crisis Text Line is helping teens is by sharing the _____

_____

so that organizations can _____

_____

Another way the service is helping teens is by building _____

_____

so that they can _____

2. Why do you think teens reach out to the service most often between 11 p.m. and 4 a.m.?

Teens might reach out most often between 11 p.m. and 4 a.m. because that is when they

_____

_____

Teens might also contact Crisis Text Line late at night because they are _____

_____

_____

ANALYZE CRAFT & STRUCTURE
Use the frames to analyze the speaker's word choices.

3. Host Nora Young says, ". . . it made them realize there was a dire need for a large-scale crisis counseling service aimed directly at teens who text." What is the meaning of the word *dire*? What context clues helped you determine the meaning?

The meaning of the word *dire* is _____

The context clues that helped me determine the meaning are that it is used as

_____

and _____

4. Young asks, "What kinds of patterns or insights have emerged that you're able to use to help teenagers using the service?" Is this a strong question? Why or why not?

This (is/is not) _____ a strong question because it _____

_____

_____

The question allows the person who is being interviewed the chance to _____

_____

_____

_____

Words to Go

BUILD WORD KNOWLEDGE

Complete the meaning and examples for this high-utility academic word.

Word to Go	Meaning	Examples
crisis cri•sis *noun*	a time of severe emotional _____ or _____	When I was in **crisis**, I really needed _____ _____ Ava was going through a **crisis** because her _____ _____ _____

DISCUSS & WRITE EXAMPLES

Discuss your response with a partner. Then complete the sentence in writing.

The school counselor helps students in times of **crisis** by _____

_____

Write your response and read it aloud to a partner. Listen and record a new idea.

Many people were in _____ after the _____

_____

BUILD WORD KNOWLEDGE

Complete the meanings and examples for these high-utility academic words.

Words to Go	Meanings	Examples
counseling coun•sel•ing *noun*	_____ given to people about their _____	If I had problems with _____ _____ _____ I would consider getting **counseling**.
counselor coun•sel•or *noun*	someone who offers _____ with problems	My uncle went to a **counselor** who helped him _____ _____

DISCUSS & WRITE EXAMPLES

Discuss your response with a partner. Then complete the sentence in writing.

After the earthquake, many students needed **counseling** because they felt _____

_____

Write your response and read it aloud to a partner. Listen and record a new idea.

The _____ at our school helps students with issues such as _____

Classmate's Name	Idea for *Crisis*	Idea for *Counselor/Counseling*

Close Reading

BUILD FLUENCY

Read "In Texting Era, Crisis Hotlines Put Help at Youths' Fingertips" (*Issues,* pp. 57–61).

IDENTIFY KEY IDEAS & DETAILS

Take turns asking and answering questions with a partner. Then write brief notes.

Discussion Frames	Text Notes
Q: What is this text **primarily about**? **A:** This text is **primarily about** _____.	• how texting has become a tool for _____ _____
Q: What are the **most essential details** in this text? **A:** (One/An additional) **essential detail** in this text is _____. **A:** Perhaps the **most essential detail** in this text is _____.	• counseling by _____ is still more common but texting is the way most teens _____ • texting can be a useful tool because it is _____ and teens can _____ • crisis text conversations tend to be _____ and _____

RESPOND WITH EVIDENCE

Use the frame and text evidence to compare texts.

1. The news article and the podcast both discuss Crisis Text Line. What is a benefit of texting explained in the news article but not the podcast?

   One benefit of texting explained in the news article but not the podcast is that texting allows teens to _____

   _____

Use the frame to analyze text structure.

2. How does the author develop the idea that texting is an effective form of counseling?

   The author develops the idea that texting is an effective form of counseling by comparing texting to _____

   Leslie Kaufman notes that people who text receive the same _____ _____

   Then she points out that texting is different because texters often _____ _____

IDENTIFY PRECISE WORDS

Review Text 3 and your *Portfolio* (pp. 126–129) to identify words for your writing.

Domain-Specific Topic Words	High-Utility Academic Words
• crisis counselor • •	• prevalent • •

Student Writing Model

Academic Writing Type

An **informative text** examines a topic and conveys ideas and information without including personal opinions.

A. The **introduction** identifies the topic and contains a thesis statement that tells what the writer will explain.

B. **Important details** develop the topic with text evidence. Evidence can include facts, statistics, examples, and quotations.

C. The **conclusion** follows from the information presented and explains the topic's importance.

D. **Transition words or phrases** connect ideas and show relationships.

ANALYZE TEXT STRUCTURE

Read this student model to analyze the elements of an informative essay.

A
Recent studies on adolescent interaction indicate that the technology of texting is profoundly changing the way teens communicate. Because cell phones are common among teens, researchers have noticed specific practices that texters rely on to communicate quickly and to develop ties with others.

B1
One clear result of texting is the growing use of improper grammar. Due to texting's rapid-fire nature, teens often omit punctuation (Fisher 56). In contrast to other forms of communication, texting is less formal.

B2
Another consequence of texting is that many teens use it to donate to charities. According to Nieman Journalism Lab, about one in five people ages 18–29 use text donations (49). Perhaps the most significant outcome is that texting allows people to write more like they speak. For example, texters do not have to consider capitalization or punctuation (Fisher 56).

C
These findings suggest that texting is altering communication in ways that are dramatic and sometimes alarming.

MARK & DISCUSS ELEMENTS

Mark the informative text elements and discuss them with your partner.

1. **Put brackets around the thesis statement.** *The thesis statement is _____.*

2. **Draw a box around three transition words or phrases.**
   One transition (word/phrase) is _____. Another transition (word/phrase) is _____.

3. **Underline three important details.** *One important detail is _____.*

4. **Label three pieces of evidence that develop the topic with the letter *E*.**
   One piece of evidence that develops the topic is _____.

5. **Star four precise topic words and check four high-utility academic words.** *An example of a (precise topic word/high-utility academic word) is _____.*

Language for Quantity & Frequency

Reason (Why?)	Quantity (How many?)	Frequency (How often?)	Examples
because since due to as a result of	none few some several many most nearly all every	never rarely occasionally regularly frequently usually constantly always	**Most** teens send texts rather than call, **since** they can **frequently** text while doing something else. **As a result of** the popularity of texting, **many** charities now **regularly** raise money through text donations. Teens **constantly** use "textisms" **because** they allow **some** teens to express themselves quickly and accurately.

USE PRECISE LANGUAGE

Rewrite each pair of simple sentences as a complex sentence, using the reason, quantity, and frequency words in parentheses.

Simple Sentences: Nancy Lublin established the Crisis Text Line.
Teens began texting about their problems.

Complex Sentence: Nancy Lublin established the Crisis Text Line **because some** teens began **occasionally** texting about their problems.

1. Teens use informal language in texts. Parents worry about teens' writing skills. *(due to, nearly all, frequently)*

_____

_____

_____

2. Texting mimics the way people speak. We use proper grammar in texts. *(since, most, rarely)*

_____

_____

_____

3. Teens have strong informal writing abilities. Teens use textisms. *(as a result of, many, regularly)*

_____

_____

_____

4. Teens prefer texting. Texting is more direct. *(because, some, always)*

_____

_____

_____

Using Homophones Correctly

Commonly Used Homophones	
to/too/two	*there/their/they're*
to: in the direction of	**there:** at or in a place
too: also; very	**their:** belonging to them
two: the number between 1 and 3	**they're:** contraction for they are
who's/whose	*it's/its*
who's: contraction for who is	**it's:** contraction for it is
whose: belonging to whom	**its:** belonging to it

 IDENTIFY HOMOPHONES

Circle the homophone errors. Write the correct word above.

> Recent studies on adolescent technology use indicate that 96% of young adults own a cell phone, and their using them to communicate in a variety of ways. Researchers have found that teens are using cell phones too text, play games, post updates to there social networks, and keep up with whose doing what in the world. They also use cell phones for making calls, but not nearly as much as they do for texting.
>
> One clear impact of smartphone use is that its reducing the amount of time that teens once had for self-contemplation. Perhaps young adults think two much time for reflection is negative because studies have shown that teens would prefer Internet access to having a car.
>
> These findings lead researchers to observe that their is a sense of freedom for teens who's primary form of communication is a phone.

 WRITE HOMOPHONES

Choose the correct homophones to complete each sentence.

1. Many teens feel anxious if (there/their/they're) _____ away from (there/their/they're) _____ smartphones for too long.

2. Teens (who's/whose) _____ writing skills are strong are likely to code switch easily between formal and informal writing.

3. Some worry that (to/too/two) _____ much texting is distracting.

4. Crisis Text Line plans to share (it's/its) _____ data with the public.

5. A teen (who's/whose) _____ in distress can text privately.

Organize an Informative Text

Prompt	How is texting affecting the way we communicate? Write an informative text that provides important details to develop the topic.

Transitions to Clarify Relationships	Examples

Cause/Effect
 	
One (impact/consequence) of _____
    is _____.
 	
Another (effect/result) of _____
    is _____.
 	
Because _____, _____.
 	
Due to _____, _____.
 	
Compare/Contrast
 	
Similarly, _____.
 	
However, _____.
 	
In contrast to _____, _____.
 	
Unlike _____, _____.
	One impact of changing technology **is** that more teens text every day than talk on their phones every day.
	
	Due to new forms of communication, local 911 services are changing the ways people can report emergencies.
	
	Similarly, the use of "LOL" to show empathy rather than mean someone is actually laughing shows that texting is creating a new language.
	
	In contrast to the long history of spoken language, using writing to communicate is a much more recent development.

IDENTIFY TRANSITIONS

Review the transitions that writers use to clarify relationships. Then complete each sentence below with an appropriate transition.

1. _____ so many teens texted about problems, Lublin started the Crisis Text Line.

2. _____ that teens can contact the hotline 24/7.

3. _____ teens most want someone to listen to them.

PLAN KEY IDEAS & DETAILS

Write a thesis statement that tells what you will explain about the topic.

Recent studies on adolescent interaction _____ that technology
    (citation verb: suggest, indicate, demonstrate)

is _____ changing the ways teens communicate.
    (adverb: dramatically, profoundly, significantly)

List three important details to develop the topic with text evidence.

1. _____

    _____

    _____

2. _____

    _____

    _____

3. _____

    _____

    _____

Write an Informative Text

Prompt How is texting affecting the way we communicate? Write an informative text that provides important details to develop the topic.

WRITE A RESEARCH PAPER
Use the frame to write an introduction, important details, and conclusion.

A

Recent studies on adolescent interaction _____ that
(citation verb: suggest, indicate, demonstrate)

technology is _____ changing the way teens communicate.
(adverb: drastically, profoundly, significantly)

Because cell phones are _____ among teens, researchers
(adjective: common, widespread, prevalent)

have noticed _____ practices that teens rely on to
(adjective: specific, particular, predictable)

communicate _____ with others.
(adverb: quickly, competently, effectively)

B1

One clear _____ of texting is the growing use
(noun: result, consequence, impact, outcome)

of _____
(noun phrase)

_____ the rapid-fire nature of texting, teens
(transition to clarify relationships)

often _____
(present-tense verb: leave out words, omit punctuation, use shortcuts)

_____ when they text _____
(citation)

_____ other forms of communication, this practice may
(transition to clarify relationships)

make texting seem (more/less) _____ _____
(adjective: casual, scholarly, formal)

B2

Another _____ consequence of
(adjective: positive, negative, remarkable, surprising)

_____ texting instead of face-to-face communication is that
(adjective: consistent, chronic, daily, obsessive)

many teens _____
(present-tense verb: interact, donate, express, seek)

According to _____
(title of text or name of source)

this results in _____
(evidence from text)

_____

Perhaps the most _____ practice researchers
(adjective: significant, impressive, dramatic)

have observed is that texting has become a way for young people

to _____
(base verb: donate, write, speak, reach out, seek)

_____

For example, young people can _____
(evidence from text)

_____

C

These findings _____ that texting is
(citation verb: prove, demonstrate, indicate)

_____ communication in ways that are
(verb + –ing: changing, affecting, altering)

_____ and _____
(adjective: impressive, dramatic, significant, widespread) _(adjective: beneficial, alarming, serious, worrisome)_

Rate Your Informative Text

ASSESS YOUR DRAFT
Mark the elements in your informative text.

1. Put brackets around the thesis statement.

2. Draw a box around three transition words or phrases.

3. Underline three important details.

4. Label three pieces of evidence that develop the topic with the letter *E*.

5. Star four precise topic words and check four high-utility academic words.

Scoring Guide
① **Insufficient**
② **Developing**
③ **Sufficient**
④ **Exemplary**

Rate your informative text. Then have a partner rate it.

1. Does the introduction contain a thesis statement that tells what you will explain about the topic?	Self	① ② ③ ④
	Partner	① ② ③ ④
2. Do the important details develop the topic with text evidence, including facts, statistics, examples, or quotations?	Self	① ② ③ ④
	Partner	① ② ③ ④
3. Did you use transitions to show relationships and connect ideas?	Self	① ② ③ ④
	Partner	① ② ③ ④
4. Did you include precise topic words and high-utility academic words?	Self	① ② ③ ④
	Partner	① ② ③ ④
5. Does the conclusion sum up and restate the thesis about the topic?	Self	① ② ③ ④
	Partner	① ② ③ ④

REFLECT & REVISE
Record specific priorities and suggestions to help you and your partner revise.

(Partner) Positive Feedback: You did an effective job of (using/including/explaining)

_____

(Partner) Suggestion: Your informative text will be stronger if you (include/improve/explain) _____

(Self) Priority 1: I will revise my informative text so that it (includes/develops/explains)

_____

(Self) Priority 2: I also need to (add/revise/check) _____

_____

CHECK & EDIT
Use this checklist to proofread and edit your informative text.

☐ Did you capitalize text titles and proper nouns?

☐ Did you format citations correctly?

☐ Did you use homophones correctly?

☐ Is each sentence complete?

☐ Are all words spelled correctly?

What makes someone a GOOD FRIEND?

 BUILD KNOWLEDGE
Read the overview (*Issues*, p. 62).

 BRAINSTORM IDEAS
Write a quick list of ways that your friends support you.

- attend events I participate in (A) _____
- _____

- _____
- _____

 EXCHANGE IDEAS
Use the frames to discuss ideas with your group. Listen attentively and record the strongest ideas to complete the chart.

> **Language to FACILITATE DISCUSSION**
> So, _____, what are your thoughts?
> _____, what idea can you add?

1. One example of something my friends (do/ say) to support me is _____ (**verb + –ing:** helping)

2. Another way my friends support me is by _____ (**verb + –ing**)

3. My friends often (do/say) things like _____ (**verb + –ing**)

4. When I have a difficult day, my close friends help by _____ (**verb + –ing**)

ACTIONS	WORDS
• help with school projects	• tell me I'm okay
•	•
•	•
•	•

Words to Know

BUILD WORD KNOWLEDGE

Rate your word knowledge. Then discuss word meanings and examples with your group.

Language to COMPARE

Our example builds upon _____'s group's.

	① Don't Know	② Recognize	③ Familiar	④ Know

Words to Know	Meanings	Examples
1 **admire** *verb* ①②③④	to _____ someone or something's qualities	I always **admire** the many _____ that I see at the _____ Many people stood in their front yards to **admire** the _____
2 **adoringly** *adverb* ①②③④	in a way that shows great _____ or devotion	Couples in movies are always staring **adoringly** into each other's eyes and saying, "_____ " When my little sister looked **adoringly** at _____ we knew that we should get it for her.
3 **chorus** *noun* ①②③④	the part of a _____ a singer _____ after each verse	Remembering the **chorus** of my favorite song is easy because I hear it _____ _____ _____ The _____ _____ joined in to sing the song's **chorus**.
4 **predator** *noun* ①②③④	an animal that _____ other animals for _____	The new movie about jungle **predators** will probably show _____ _____ _____ The **predator** I would be most frightened to encounter is a _____ _____

Language to FACILITATE DISCUSSION

I've never seen or heard the word _____.

I recognize the word _____ but need to learn how to use it.

I can use _____ in a sentence. For example, _____.

I know the word _____. It means _____.

We are unfamiliar with the word _____.

We recognize the word _____, but we would benefit from a review of (the meaning/how to use it in a sentence).

We think _____ means _____.

Building Concepts

DEVELOP UNDERSTANDING
Complete the organizer to build your knowledge of the concept.

relationship *(noun)*

Example Sentence

My sister and I argue sometimes, but we have a close **relationship** and she can usually **relate** when I have a problem.

Synonyms		Word Family
Everyday:	Precise:	• relationship *(noun)*
• _____	• _____	• relate *(verb)*
• _____	• _____	• relation *(noun)*
		• related *(adjective)*

Meaning

the way that people _____ about and _____ toward each other

Essential Characteristics

• people or things that _____ each other

• the closeness you have with people in your _____

Examples

• feeling close to your parents

• _____
_____
_____
_____

• _____
_____
_____
_____

Non-Examples

• passing a stranger on the street

• _____
_____
_____
_____

• _____
_____
_____
_____

Write About It

Developing a close **relationship** with a friend can be challenging *because you have to*

_____

However, **relationships** *are important because they provide* _____

_____

Words to Know

Language to COMPARE

Our example builds upon _____'s group's.

BUILD WORD KNOWLEDGE

Rate your word knowledge. Then discuss word meanings and examples with your group.

	① Don't Know	② Recognize	③ Familiar	④ Know

Words to Know	Meanings	Examples
1 **enchanted** *adjective* ①②③④	changed by _____ or something beautiful	If I had an **enchanted** _____ I could easily _____ _____ **Enchanted** by the gorgeous _____ we were unwilling to _____ _____
2 **insult** *verb* ①②③④	to say or do something _____ or disrespectful	I didn't mean to **insult** my friend when I said that (his/her) _____ Ezra **insulted** his friend by _____ _____
3 **kingdom** *noun* ①②③④	one of the _____ into which living things are _____; a country ruled by a _____	Lea's fascination with the animal **Kingdom** has led her to study _____ _____ As the ruler of a **Kingdom**, I would _____ _____ _____
4 **stronghold** *noun* ①②③④	a place that is _____ against _____ _____ or danger	My brother believes that his room is a **stronghold**, so he put _____ _____ In the video game, you can enter the castle **stronghold** only after you _____ _____ _____

Language to FACILITATE DISCUSSION

I've never seen or heard the word _____.

I recognize the word _____ but need to learn how to use it.

I can use _____ in a sentence. For example, _____.

I know the word _____. It means _____.

We are unfamiliar with the word _____.

We recognize the word _____, but we would benefit from a review of (the meaning/how to use it in a sentence).

We think _____ means _____.

Academic Discussion

What are the characteristics of a good friend?

BRAINSTORM IDEAS

Briefly record at least two ideas in each column using everyday English.

Individual Qualities	Social Qualities
• listens when you speak • • •	• helps you with problems • • •

ANALYZE LANGUAGE

Complete the chart with precise words to discuss and write about the topic.

Everyday	Precise
good *(adjective)*	loyal,
nice *(adjective)*	compassionate,
easy to talk to *(adjective)*	receptive,

MAKE A CLAIM

Rewrite an idea using the frames and precise words.
Then prepare to elaborate verbally.

Frame: In my experience, a good friend is someone who is
_____ (**adjective:** honest, supportive) and _____
(**adjective:** dependable, respectful)

Response: _____

_____

_____

_____

Language to ELABORATE

For example, _____.

This is the case because _____.

EXCHANGE IDEAS

Listen attentively, restate, and record your partner's idea.

Classmate's Name	Idea

Language to RESTATE

So your perspective is that _____.

Yes, that's correct.

No, not exactly. What I meant was _____.

Ten-Minute Response

A **ten-minute response** uses academic register. It begins with a well-stated **claim**, followed by **two detail sentences** that elaborate with relevant examples and precise words.

PRESENT IDEAS

Listen attentively and take notes. Then indicate if you agree (+) or disagree (–).

Language to AGREE/DISAGREE

I (agree/disagree) with _____'s perspective.

Classmate's Name	Idea	+/–

Prompt What are the characteristics of a good friend? Write a ten-minute response that states and supports your claim.

ELABORATE IN WRITING

Work with the teacher to write a ten-minute response in academic register.

Language to COLLABORATE

What should we write? We could try _____.

Do you agree? Another option is _____.

Okay. Let's write _____.

In my experience, a good friend is someone who is fair and open. For example, friends may have (a/an) _____ topic to discuss, such as (a/an)

_____

Therefore, good friends must _____ and _____

_____

so that they can _____

_____

Write a ten-minute response on your own using academic register.

In my experience, a good friend is someone who is _____

and _____ For example, I may go through (a/an)

_____ experience, such as _____

_____

Therefore, I would want my good friend to _____

and _____

_____

Words to Go

BUILD WORD KNOWLEDGE

Complete the meanings and examples
for these high-utility academic words.

> **Language to LISTEN ACTIVELY**
>
> What example did you appreciate?
> I appreciated _____'s example, _____.
>
> What example did you relate to?
> I related to _____'s example, _____.

Words to Go	Meanings	Examples
emphatic em•phat•ic *adjective*	_____ and strong	When I get home from school, I have to _____ because my father is **emphatic** about being clean.
emphatically em•phat•i•cal•ly *adverb*	doing something with great energy or _____	Kashana didn't see me, so I _____ _____ **emphatically** until she did.

DISCUSS & WRITE EXAMPLES

Discuss your response with a partner. Then complete the sentence in writing.

My sister was **emphatic** in saying that I couldn't go with her last night,

so I _____

Write your response and read it aloud to a partner. Listen and record a new idea.

I _____ agreed to go to the _____

because I really wanted to _____

BUILD WORD KNOWLEDGE

Complete the meaning and examples for this high-utility academic word.

Word to Go	Meaning	Examples
expression ex•pres•sion *noun*	the _____ on someone's face that shows what he or she is _____ or _____	The **expression** on my grandmother's face when I _____ told me that I was in trouble. Coach had an angry **expression** when Sam

DISCUSS & WRITE EXAMPLES

Discuss your response with a partner. Then complete the sentence in writing.

I could tell from Jade's **expression** that she was _____ with

her _____

Write your response and read it aloud to a partner. Listen and record a new idea.

I'm sure the _____ on my face looked _____

after I spent all weekend working on my _____

Classmate's Name	Idea for *Emphatic/Emphatically*	Idea for *Expression*

Close Reading

 READ THE TEXT

Read Section 1 of "Bridge to Terabithia: A Play With Music" (*Issues,* pp. 63–67).

IDENTIFY STRUCTURE

> **Dramatic Structure**
>
> Most dramas include **stage directions** that usually appear in italic type inside parentheses. Stage directions tell actors what to do and give information about characters' feelings and actions.

Use the frames to analyze the drama's stage directions.

1. What do the stage directions reveal about how the relationship between Leslie and Jesse changes after they sing the song together?

    One stage direction that shows Leslie and Jesse's relationship before singing the

    song is _____

    _____

    A stage direction that shows how Jesse and Leslie's relationship (improves/worsens)

    _____ after singing the song is _____

    _____

2. How do the stage directions show that Leslie is different from other girls in the class?

    The stage directions show that Leslie _____

    This reveals that Leslie is (more/less) _____ concerned about

    _____

    _____

RESPOND WITH EVIDENCE
Use the frames to analyze the author's word choice.

3. Why does the author use the word *elaborately* to describe how Janice applies hand lotion?

    The author uses the word *elaborately* to describe the way Janice applies hand lotion to show

    that Janice sees herself as _____ and is not focused

    on what is _____

    _____

ANALYZE THEME
Use the frames to analyze the drama's theme.

4. How does the song the class sings contribute to the drama's theme so far?

    The song the class sings contributes to the drama's theme of _____

    _____

    Both Jesse and Leslie feel _____ in their schools, and the song is a way

    for them to _____

Words to Go

BUILD WORD KNOWLEDGE
Complete the meaning and examples
for this high-utility academic word.

Word to Go	Meaning	Examples
priority pri•or•i•ty *noun*	something that is more _____ than other things	Having good health is a **priority** for me, so I try to _____ _____ _____ should be my **priority** when I get home from school.

DISCUSS & WRITE EXAMPLES
Discuss your response with a partner. Then complete the sentence in writing.

Many teens' top **priorities** are _____

and _____

Write your response and read it aloud to a partner. Listen and record a new idea.

One _____ for the student council is _____

_____

BUILD WORD KNOWLEDGE
Complete the meanings and examples for these high-utility academic words.

Words to Go	Meanings	Examples
assess as•sess *verb*	to _____ at an event in order to learn from it	After _____ the landlord came back home to **assess** the damage.
reassess re•as•sess *verb*	to think about something _____	When Tony got his report card, he knew that he had to **reassess** his _____ _____

DISCUSS & WRITE EXAMPLES
Discuss your response with a partner. Then complete the sentence in writing.

If I want to sign up for that _____ I'll need to

assess if I _____

Write your response and read it aloud to a partner.

After I found out that I had two essays due the same day, I _____

my _____

Classmate's Name	Idea for *Priority*	Idea for *Assess/Reassess*

Close Reading

READ THE TEXT

Read Section 2 of "Bridge to Terabithia: A Play With Music" (*Issues,* pp. 67–70).

IDENTIFY KEY IDEAS & DETAILS

Use the frames to make inferences and analyze key details.

1. What inference can you make about Leslie's relationship with her parents?

   Leslie refers to her parents as _____ instead of

   _____

   _____

   This implies that Leslie's relationship with her parents is _____

2. What does Jesse and Leslie's conversation about drawing reveal?

   One important moment that takes place between Jesse and Leslie is when Leslie

   _____

   _____

   Leslie goes on to mention _____

   to show Jesse that art is _____

ANALYZE CRAFT & STRUCTURE

> ### Dramatic Elements
>
> **Dialogue** is the words that characters speak in a play or story. In dramas, dialogue follows the name of the character. Authors use dialogue to develop characters—as characters speak, they come alive, and readers learn who they are.

Use the frames to analyze dialogue and character development.

3. What dialogue reveals what Leslie believes about how animals should be treated?

   Leslie reveals an opinion about animals when she _____

   _____

   _____

   This shows that she believes that people _____

   _____

   _____

4. Why does the author include Leslie's opinions about how animals should be treated?

   The author includes Leslie's opinions on how animals should be treated to show that

   Leslie _____

   _____

   and that she is a person who _____

   _____

Words to Go

BUILD WORD KNOWLEDGE
Complete the meaning and examples for this high-utility academic word.

Language to LISTEN ACTIVELY

What example did you appreciate?
I appreciated _____'s example, _____.

What example did you relate to?
I related to _____'s example, _____.

Word to Go	Meaning	Examples
ruler ru•ler *noun*	someone with _____ over _____ _____	Good **rulers** make sure to _____ _____ The movie was about evil **rulers** who cared only about _____

DISCUSS & WRITE EXAMPLES
Discuss your response with a partner. Then complete the sentence in writing.

After Jacob didn't _____

he joked that he should be **ruler** of _____

Write your response and read it aloud to a partner. Listen and record a new idea.

The _____ of each disputing country met to discuss how to

_____

BUILD WORD KNOWLEDGE
Complete the meaning and examples for this high-utility academic word.

Word to Go	Meaning	Examples
collaborate col•lab•or•ate *verb*	to work _____ to do something	In science class, we often **collaborate** on _____ _____ My sister and I **collaborated** to _____ _____ because the job was too much to do _____

DISCUSS & WRITE EXAMPLES
Discuss your response with a partner. Then complete the sentence in writing.

Liam and Sofia have the same _____

so they are **collaborating** to _____

Write your response and read it aloud to a partner. Listen and record a new idea.

Two of my favorite _____ are planning to _____

to _____

Classmate's Name	Idea for *Ruler*	Idea for *Collaborate*

Close Reading

READ THE TEXT
Read Section 3 of "Bridge to Terabithia: A Play With Music" (*Issues,* pp. 70–72).

IDENTIFY KEY IDEAS & DETAILS
Use the frames to make inferences and analyze key details.

1. Does Leslie think less of Jesse because he hasn't read the books or heard of the magical creatures she mentions? How do you know?

   Leslie (does/does not) _____ think less of Jesse because she

   _____

   and that she will _____

   Then she _____

   and says that Jesse will _____

ANALYZE CRAFT & STRUCTURE

> ### Setting
> The **setting** is where and when a story takes place. Think about how the setting influences events and affects the characters and mood.

Use the frames to identify and analyze the drama's setting.

2. What is the setting of this section of the drama?

   The setting of this section is the _____

   _____

   _____

3. How does the setting affect the story?

   In the classroom, Leslie and Jesse are aware of how _____

   _____

   However, in this _____ setting, they can be _____ too.

ANALYZE THEME
Use the frames to analyze the drama's theme.

4. How does Leslie's line, "It would be so secret that we would never tell anyone in the whole world about it" contribute to the drama's theme?

   Leslie's line emphasizes the idea that Jesse and Leslie feel _____

   with each other, which is an important part of _____

   _____

   This contributes to the drama's theme that it is important to _____

   _____

   _____

Analyze an Audiobook

▶ **COMPARE MEDIA**

Listen to the audiobook *Bridge to Terabithia*. Use the frames to discuss ideas with your partner.

1. I appreciate how the reader _____.

2. Unlike the drama, the audiobook _____.

✏ **LISTEN & TAKE NOTES**

Listen to the audiobook again. Listen closely and complete the outline.

I. Leslie and Jesse find a _____

that hangs from _____ over a _____

  A. Both Jesse and Leslie take turns _____

  B. When Jesse looks up while _____

    he feels like he is _____

II. Leslie decides that she and Jesse need a place that is _____

_____

It will be like _____

_____

  A. Jesse feels excited at the idea of _____

  B. Leslie tells Jesse that the new land could be _____

  _____

    i. Leslie says they can only enter the land by _____

    _____

III. Jesse and Leslie run through the woods to _____

  A. Jesse is _____ to enter the woods, but he keeps telling Leslie

  _____

  B. Leslie looks for a place where the ground is _____ and

  _____

    i. Leslie finds _____

    _____

    then she calls the land _____

Language to COMPARE
What caught my attention was _____.
I particularly noted the fact that _____.
Like _____, I appreciated the way the reader _____.

Close Listening

IDENTIFY KEY IDEAS & DETAILS
Use the frames to analyze key details.

1. How does Jesse feel when he swings from the rope? How does it compare to Jesse's feelings as he explores the woods with Leslie?

   When Jesse swings from the rope, it is as though he is _____

   _____

   which means Jesse feels _____ while swinging. Later, when he

   explores the woods with Leslie, Jesse feels _____

   _____ because they make him feel like he's _____

2. How does Leslie show her feelings when she and Jesse explore the woods?

   When Leslie and Jesse explore the woods, Leslie shows her feelings by _____

   _____

   _____

   and _____

   _____

   _____

   These details indicate that Leslie is _____ about the imaginary land.

INTEGRATE IDEAS

> ### Tone
>
> **Tone** is the attitude an author shows toward a text's themes and narrow subject matter. The tone can be anything the author chooses: serious or humorous, formal or informal. An author usually shows tone through dialogue, description, and narration.

Use the frames to analyze how the audiobook's tone compares to the drama.

3. When Jesse and Leslie discover the rope swing, how does the tone of the audiobook differ from the tone of the drama?

   When Jesse and Leslie discover the rope swing, the tone of the audiobook is _____

   _____

   The audiobook describes the autumn day as _____ and

   states Jesse feels like he's _____ The tone of the drama is

   _____ because the drama's specific details _____

   _____

   _____

Academic Discussion

What strengthens relationships?

BRAINSTORM IDEAS
Briefly record at least two ideas in each column using everyday English.

Interests	Experiences
• liking the same books	• going on a trip together
•	•
•	•
•	•

ANALYZE LANGUAGE
Complete the chart with precise words to discuss and write about the topic.

Everyday	Precise
same *(adjective)*	comparable,
having *(verb)*	encountering,
telling *(verb)*	disclosing,

MAKE A CLAIM
Rewrite an idea using the frame and precise words.
Then prepare to elaborate verbally.

Frame: People strengthen their relationships by _____
(**verb** + *–ing:* sharing, trusting, finding, developing)

Response: _____

_____

_____

_____

_____

_____

Language to ELABORATE

For example, _____.

This is the case because
_____.

EXCHANGE IDEAS
Listen attentively, restate, and record your partner's idea.

Classmate's Name	Idea

Language to RESTATE

So your perspective is
that _____.

Yes, that's correct.

No, not exactly. What I
meant was _____.

Ten-Minute Response

A **ten-minute response** uses academic register. It begins with a well-stated **claim,** followed by **two detail sentences** that elaborate with relevant examples and precise words.

PRESENT IDEAS
Listen attentively and take notes. Then indicate if you agree (+) or disagree (–).

Language to AGREE/DISAGREE

I (agree/ disagree) with _____'s perspective.

Classmate's Name	Idea	+/–

Prompt	What strengthens relationships? Write a ten-minute response that states and supports your claim.

ELABORATE IN WRITING
Work with the teacher to write a ten-minute response in academic register.

Language to COLLABORATE

What should we write? We could try _____.

Do you agree? Another option is _____.

Okay. Let's write _____.

People strengthen their relationships by experiencing comparable hardships.

For example, two friends might both _____

_____

As a result, they both feel that they can _____

_____

without _____

Write a ten-minute response on your own using academic register.

People strengthen their relationships by _____

_____

For example, shortly after I met my best friend, I found out that (he/she) _____

had (a/an) _____

_____

As a result, we _____

and we _____

_____

Language to LISTEN ACTIVELY

What example did you appreciate?
I appreciated _____'s example.

What example did you relate to?
I related to _____'s example.

Words to Go

BUILD WORD KNOWLEDGE

Complete the meanings and examples for this high-utility academic word.

Word to Go	Meanings	Examples
complicated com•pli•cat•ed *adjective*	_____ to understand; having _____ different parts or ideas	Having too many friends makes deciding _____ _____ **complicated**. Planning the group project is **complicated** because I want to _____ _____ _____

DISCUSS & WRITE EXAMPLES

Discuss your response with a partner. Then complete the sentence in writing.

My decision to _____

was **complicated** because I _____

Write your response and read it aloud to a partner. Listen and record a new idea.

My life gets quite _____ when my two best friends _____

_____

BUILD WORD KNOWLEDGE

Complete the meaning and examples for this high-utility academic word.

Word to Go	Meaning	Examples
negotiate neg•o•ti•ate *verb*	to discuss something in order to reach an _____ or _____	I tried to **negotiate** with my teacher for _____ but it didn't work. My _____ and I **negotiated** for half an hour before we agreed on _____

DISCUSS & WRITE EXAMPLES

Discuss your response with a partner. Then complete the sentence in writing.

The student council **negotiated** with the principal so that students would be allowed to

_____

Write your response and read it aloud to a partner. Listen and record a new idea.

My aunt is always _____ with me so I'll _____

_____

Classmate's Name	Idea for *Complicated*	Idea for *Negotiate*

Close Reading

READ THE TEXT

Read the text "Our Good Day" (*Issues,* pp. 73–75).

IDENTIFY KEY IDEAS & DETAILS

> ### Repetition
>
> **Repetition** is repeating specific words or phrases again and again. Authors use repetition to show the importance of an idea or to add style and engage the audience.

Use the frame to analyze the author's use of repetition.

1. What word and phrase does the author repeat at the beginning of "Our Good Day"? What does the repetition emphasize about Esperanza?

   The author repeats the phrase _____

   The repetition emphasizes that Esperanza _____

   _____

ANALYZE CRAFT & STRUCTURE

> ### Figurative Language
>
> A **simile** compares two things using the words *like* or *as.* Similes are a type of imagery that helps readers picture what they are reading.

Use the frame to analyze the author's use of simile.

2. Cathy says that Lucy and Rachel "smell like a broom." What does the simile suggest about what Cathy thinks of the girls?

   The author uses the simile "smell like a broom" to suggest that Cathy has a

   (positive/negative) _____ opinion of Lucy and Rachel because they

   are _____ and _____

Use the frame to analyze the author's treatment of dialogue.

3. Sandra Cisneros does not set the characters' dialogue inside quotation marks. What effect does this have?

   Cisneros writes dialogue without using quotation marks to make the text look

   _____ and _____ She wants the text to be

   _____

ANALYZE THEME

Use the frame to analyze the story's theme.

4. How does "when I tell them my name they don't laugh" contribute to the story's theme?

   The text "when I tell them my name they don't laugh" shows that Lucy and Rachel

   _____

   It reinforces the theme of Esperanza's struggle with her _____

   while emphasizing the importance of _____ among friends.

Student Writing Model

Academic Writing Type

A **narrative** tells a story from a clear point of view. Narratives can be imagined events or true experiences written from someone's life.

   A. The **topic sentence** clearly identifies the purpose of the narrative.

   B. **Detail sentences** describe a sequence of events using action verbs and sensory details.

   C. The **conclusion** explains the importance of the story.

   D. **Transition words or phrases** help move the reader through the events of the story.

ANALYZE TEXT STRUCTURE
Read this student model to analyze the elements of a narrative.

A

I first met Malcolm when we were 12 years old and played on the school soccer team. At that time, we didn't have an immediate and powerful connection. However, several weeks later an experience drastically changed my perspective about Malcolm.

B1

It all began when we were competing against my old school. My old rival was on their team, and he was bragging about how he always used to beat me at sports. Suddenly, Malcolm decided to give up the perfect chance to score the winning goal. He passed the ball to me, and I made the goal instead! I was surprised that he was so selfless. It made me realize that Malcolm was more than a classmate. In fact, he was a conscientious and amazing friend.

B2

Since that day, my relationship with Malcolm has continued to grow. We continue to spend time playing soccer and taking guitar lessons. Our friendship is an anchor in my life.

C

Even though we didn't have an immediate connection, I hope we will remain devoted friends. For now, we are as close as a goalie and his shin guards.

MARK & DISCUSS ELEMENTS
Mark the summary elements and use the frames to discuss them with your partner.

1. **Put brackets around the topic.** *The topic of this narrative is _____.*

2. **Draw a box around three transition words or phrases.** *One transition (word/phrase) is _____. Another transition (word/phrase) is _____.*

3. **Number events 1–5 in time order.** *The _____ event in the narrative is _____.*

4. **Star four precise adjectives and adverbs.** *An example of a precise (adjective/adverb) is _____.*

Language for Description

Guidelines for Using Language for Description

Language for description uses precise adjectives and adverbs to make writing more vivid. Sensory details help readers create images in their minds and feel like they can see, smell, hear, taste, and touch items in a story.

Everyday Descriptions	Sensory Descriptions
When I met Kaia for the first time, it was a **really nice** day, with **lots of sunshine** and a **little breeze blowing.**	When I met Kaia for the first time, it was a **glorious** day; sunbeams **poured down like gold** and a **breeze crept through the trees.**
I tried to tell Kaia **I was grateful,** but **I got all choked up** and **couldn't talk.**	I tried to tell Kaia how **immensely grateful I felt,** but **my heart filled my throat. My voice sounded smothered.**

USE DESCRIPTIVE LANGUAGE

Review the descriptive language. Then complete the narrative with appropriate descriptive and sensory language.

Everyday Language	Descriptive Language
empty	hollow, barren, useless, vacant
stinky	disgusting, smelly, reeking, musty
uncoordinated	blundering, graceless, lumbering, butterfingered
surround	clamor, horde, flock, swarm
surprisingly	refreshingly, shockingly, startlingly, stunningly
major development	miracle, godsend, marvel, phenomenon

Before I met Nicole, my social life was as _____

as a _____ I had ZERO friends. Don't get me wrong; it's not as if I

smell _____

It's just that at my school, most of the guys are _____

_____

and most of the girls _____ around them like

_____ I'm not like that at all.

But when Nicole showed up at school one day, everything changed. She was

_____ and _____

She refused to be what everyone else considered normal.

Using Pronouns Correctly

Guidelines for Using Pronouns Correctly

A **pronoun** replaces a noun or another pronoun. An **antecedent** is the noun that the pronoun replaces. A pronoun and its antecedent must agree in number (singular or plural), person (first person, second person, or third person), and gender (the masculine pronouns *he, him,* and *his;* the feminine pronouns *she* and *her;* and the neuter pronouns *it* and *its*).

*Sara and I followed **Ben,** but **we** hesitated when **he** wouldn't tell **us** the destination.*

*Miranda had heard **the song** so many times that **she** couldn't get **it** out of **her** head.*

IDENTIFY PRONOUN ERRORS
Read the narrative paragraphs and circle the pronoun errors.

> I met the twins Tomas and Thiago at his birthday party. My mother knew their mother, so she wrangled an invitation for me. You should have seen the look on her face when I told she I liked the twins a lot. Mom says a mother is always thinking about how they can improve their child's life, so she was really tickled.
>
> Tomas, Thiago, and I were hanging out one afternoon when Thiago said, "You know what we need? We need an adventure." Tomas replied, "Adventures are great but it shouldn't lead to danger." Thiago sighed and rolled his eyes. For twins, he can be really different.

WRITE PRONOUNS
Use the correct pronoun to complete each sentence.

1. Miranda gazed adoringly at the guitar, thinking about how much _____ wanted _____ as a birthday gift.

2. I don't often meet people I like right away. Usually _____ need time to figure out if _____ share my interests.

3. I cracked up when Diego and Delia bumped _____ heads during dance class.

4. Not all of my friends are alike, but _____ all make _____ feel good about _____ life.

Organize a Narrative

Prompt	Think about one of your closest friends. Write a narrative that describes when you realized that he or she was a true friend.

Transitions to Convey Sequence		Examples
first	it all began	I **first** met Noah when we were seven years old.
at that time	all at once	**At that time,** there was an enormous snowstorm.
suddenly	as	**All at once,** a snowball zinged past my head.
since then/later	now	**Since then,** Noah and I have moved on to other sports, but we remain great friends.

IDENTIFY TRANSITIONS

Review the transitions writers use to convey sequence in a narrative. Then complete the paragraph with appropriate transitions.

_____ with the discovery of a litter of kittens. The new girl,

Anne, and I were walking home when _____ we heard noise from inside

a hollow log. We couldn't take the kittens home, but we agreed to take them to the animal

shelter. As we left, Anne and I realized that we had many interests in common.

_____ we're best friends.

PLAN EVENTS & DETAILS

Use your personal experiences to write a topic sentence.

I first met (person's name) _____ when we were (number) _____

years old and were (verb + *ing:* attending, participating in, playing at) _____

_____

Describe the events you will include in your narrative. Use precise details and sensory language.

1. It all began when I was _____

_____

_____

2. Suddenly, _____

_____

_____

3. It made me realize _____

_____

_____

Write a conclusion that explains the importance of the story.

_____

_____

Write a Narrative

Prompt Think about one of your closest friends. Write a narrative that describes when you realized that he or she was a true friend.

✎ **WRITE AN ESSAY**

Use the frame to write a narrative.

A

I first met _____ when we were _____
(name)   (number)

years old and were _____
(verb + –ing: attending, participating, playing)

_____

At that time, we didn't have an immediate and _____
(adjective: strong, positive, amazing)

connection. However, several _____ later, an experience
(noun: days, weeks, years)

_____ changed my perspective about _____
(adverb: greatly, dramatically, substantially)   (name)

B1

It all began when we were _____
(verb + –ing: hiking, competing, taking)

_____

_____
(elaborate on event)

Suddenly, _____ decided to _____
(person's name)   (base verb: give, be, share)

_____

_____
(elaborate on action)

I was surprised that (he/she) _____ was so

_____ It made me realize that _____
(adjective: kind, considerate, caring)   (name)

was more than (a/an) _____ In fact, (he/she) _____
(noun: acquaintance, confidante, classmate)

might become a true and _____ friend.
(adjective: special, good, incredible)

B2

Since that day, my relationship with _____ has continued
(name)

to _____ We still spend time _____
(verb: thrive, grow, develop)   (verb + –ing: hiking, playing, attending)

and _____
(verb + –ing: playing, drawing, making)

Our friendship is like _____
(noun: an anchor, the backbone, a roller coaster)

C

Even though we didn't have an immediate connection, I hope that we will

remain _____ friends throughout
(adjective: true, loyal, constant)

_____
(time frame: scouting, middle school, our teenage years)

For now, we are as close as _____
(noun phrase to create an image: peanut butter and jelly, a stamp on a letter, milk and cookies)

Rate Your Narrative

ASSESS YOUR DRAFT
Mark the elements in your narrative.

1. Put brackets around the topic within the introduction.

2. Draw a box around three transition words or phrases.

3. Number the events of the narrative in order of time.

4. Star four precise adjectives and adverbs.

Scoring Guide
① Insufficient
② Developing
③ Sufficient
④ Exemplary

Rate your narrative. Then have a partner rate it.

1. Does the topic sentence clearly identify purpose of the narrative?	Self	① ② ③ ④
	Partner	① ② ③ ④
2. Did you use transitions to help move the reader through the story's events?	Self	① ② ③ ④
	Partner	① ② ③ ④
3. Do the detail sentences show the order of events using action verbs and sensory details?	Self	① ② ③ ④
	Partner	① ② ③ ④
4. Did you include precise verbs, adjectives, and adverbs?	Self	① ② ③ ④
	Partner	① ② ③ ④
5. Do the concluding sentences explain the importance of the story?	Self	① ② ③ ④
	Partner	① ② ③ ④

REFLECT & REVISE
Record specific priorities and suggestions to help you and your partner revise.

(Partner) Positive Feedback: You did an effective job of (using/including/explaining)

_____

(Partner) Suggestion: Your narrative will be stronger if you (include/improve/explain)

_____

(Self) Priority 1: I will revise my narrative so that it (includes/develops/explains) _____

_____

(Self) Priority 2: I also need to (add/revise/check) _____

_____

CHECK & EDIT
Use this checklist to proofread and edit your narrative.

☐ Did you capitalize proper nouns, such as people's names?

☐ Did you use commas appropriately after transitions?

☐ Did you use pronouns correctly?

☐ Is each sentence complete?

☐ Are all words spelled correctly?

Narrative Speech

| Prompt | Describe an enjoyable experience you've shared with a friend recently. Present a speech that tells a story and describes the events. |

BRAINSTORM IDEAS
Write the topic of your narrative speech.

Topic: _____

_____

ORGANIZE DETAILS
Identify the setting and events of your narrative speech.

Setting: _____

_____

Event 1: _____

_____

_____

Event 2: _____

_____

_____

WRITE A SPEECH
Write a narrative speech that includes a setting, a sequence of events, and a conclusion. Use visuals or multimedia to clarify information and add interest.

Recently, my close friend _____ and I _____

_____

_____

The _____ took place at _____

_____

We _____

_____

When _____

my friend _____

While _____

we both _____

At the end, we _____

_____

I'll always remember this experience because it was _____

_____

Present & Rate Your Speech

Ensuring Clear Pronunciation

When presenting ideas during class, use **clear pronunciation.** When you speak, make sure that you don't mumble. Pronounce sounds and words properly so that your audience understands you. For example, make sure that you say "going to" instead of "gonna."

PRESENT YOUR SPEECH

Present your speech to the small group. Make sure to use clear pronunciation.

LISTEN & TAKE NOTES

Listen attentively and take notes.

Language to AFFIRM & CLARIFY

I appreciated your story.
Could you elaborate on _____?

Classmate's Name	Idea

ASSESS YOUR SPEECH

Use the Scoring Guide to rate your speech.

Scoring Guide	
① Insufficient	② Sufficient
③ Developing	④ Exemplary

1. Did you clearly state your topic?	① ② ③ ④
2. Did you include a clear setting?	① ② ③ ④
3. Did you include sequential events?	① ② ③ ④
4. Were you easy to understand?	① ② ③ ④
5. Did you use clear pronunciation?	① ② ③ ④

REFLECT

Think of two ways you have improved on your speeches.

Praise 1: In my speeches, I was successful with (including/presenting) _____

_____

_____

Praise 2: My greatest area of improvement was (speaking/using) _____

_____

_____

Common Prefixes & Suffixes

Learn these affixes to use as clues to the meanings of unfamiliar words.

Prefix	Meaning	Examples
anti–	against	antisocial
dis–	not, opposite of	
im–, in–	not	
inter–	between	
mis–	bad, wrong	
non–, un–	not	
pre–	before	
re–	again	
sub–	below, under	
trans–	across	

Suffix	Meaning	Examples
–able, –ible (adj)	having a particular quality; something that is possible	*valuable*
–ate (verb)	to make, cause, or act	
–ation, –ion (noun)	the act or result of doing something	
–er, –or (noun)	someone who does	
–ful (adj)	full of	
–ity (noun)	having a particular quality	
–ive (adj)	having a particular quality	
–less (adj)	without	
–ly (adv)	happening in a particular way	
–ment (noun)	the result	

Completing the Daily Do Now

DAILY DO NOW ROUTINE

Follow these steps each day when you enter class:

1. **Turn** to the Daily Do Now in your *Language & Writing Portfolio* and record the date.

2. **Read** the task on the board, think carefully, and write an appropriate response.

3. **Listen** to classmates share their responses and share your response if asked.

4. **Read** your response aloud twice to your partner.

5. **Score** your response using the Scoring Guide.

SHOW YOU KNOW

Complete each Daily Do Now to show you know the word and how to use it correctly.

Example: (benefit) One of the _____ of making new friends is _____.

- Write the correct form of the word in one of the blanks. If it is a noun, you may need to make it plural (often by adding *-s* or *-es*). If it is a verb, you may need to change its tense (often by adding *-ed*, *-ing*, or *-s*).

- Complete the rest of the sentence with content that shows you understand the word's meaning.

Date _9_ / _23_ / _16_					Self
One of the benefits of making new friends is having people to sit					
with during lunch.					Teacher

Scoring the Daily Do Now

DETERMINING A SCORE

Use this rubric and the Scoring Guide to score your Daily Do Nows. Record up to two points for relevant content and one point for each of the other elements.

	Complete Do Now	Correct Word Form	Relevant Content	Correct Grammar
POINTS	1	1	2	1
Criteria	Copied the sentence and completed the blanks.	Used cues in the sentence to write the correct form of the word.	Added relevant content that shows understanding of the word meaning.	Completed the sentence using correct grammar.

CALCULATING A GRADING TOTAL

At the end of each Issue, calculate your grading total. Add up all the total points for the Issue. Calculate the possible points by multiplying the number of Daily Do Nows by 5. Then divide the total points by the possible points and multiply by 100.

	TOTAL POINTS	POSSIBLE POINTS	GRADING TOTAL (TOTAL POINTS/ POSSIBLE POINTS X 100)
Issue 1			
Issue 2			
Issue 3			
Issue 4			
Issue 5			
Issue 6			

Insufficient	Developing	Admirable	Exceptional
0–50%	51–70%	71–90%	91–100%

Daily Do Now

Record the Daily Do Now at the beginning of each class. Complete the task using the correct word form, relevant content, and correct grammar.

	Scores					
	Complete Do Now	Correct Word Form	Relevant Content	Correct Grammar	Total	

Date _____ / _____ / _____

					Self
					Teacher

Date _____ / _____ / _____

					Self
					Teacher

Date _____ / _____ / _____

					Self
					Teacher

Date _____ / _____ / _____

					Self
					Teacher

Date _____ / _____ / _____

					Self
					Teacher

Total Points

Scoring Guide

Did you **complete the Daily Do Now**?	+1
Did you **use the correct word form**?	+1
Did you add **relevant content**?	+2
Did you add content using **correct grammar**?	+1

Scores					
Complete Do Now	Correct Word Form	Relevant Content	Correct Grammar	Total	
					Self
					Teacher
					Self
					Teacher
					Self
					Teacher
					Self
					Teacher
					Self
					Teacher

Date _____ / _____ / _____

Date _____ / _____ / _____

Date _____ / _____ / _____

Date _____ / _____ / _____

Date _____ / _____ / _____

Total Points

Daily Do Now

Record the Daily Do Now at the beginning of each class. Complete the task using the correct word form, relevant content, and correct grammar.

	Scores					
	Complete Do Now	Correct Word Form	Relevant Content	Correct Grammar	Total	

| Date ____ / ____ / _____ | | | | | | Self |
| | | | | | | Teacher |

| Date ____ / ____ / _____ | | | | | | Self |
| | | | | | | Teacher |

| Date ____ / ____ / _____ | | | | | | Self |
| | | | | | | Teacher |

| Date ____ / ____ / _____ | | | | | | Self |
| | | | | | | Teacher |

| Date ____ / ____ / _____ | | | | | | Self |
| | | | | | | Teacher |

Total Points

Scoring Guide

Did you **complete the Daily Do Now**?	+1
Did you **use the correct word form**?	+1
Did you add **relevant content**?	+2
Did you add content using **correct grammar**?	+1

	Scores					
	Complete Do Now	Correct Word Form	Relevant Content	Correct Grammar	Total	
Date ____ / ____ / _____						Self
						Teacher
Date ____ / ____ / _____						Self
						Teacher
Date ____ / ____ / _____						Self
						Teacher
Date ____ / ____ / _____						Self
						Teacher
Date ____ / ____ / _____						Self
						Teacher
Total Points						

Daily Do Now

Record the Daily Do Now at the beginning of each class. Complete the task using the correct word form, relevant content, and correct grammar.

	Scores					
	Complete Do Now	Correct Word Form	Relevant Content	Correct Grammar	Total	
Date ____ / ____ / _____						Self
						Teacher
Date ____ / ____ / _____						Self
						Teacher
Date ____ / ____ / _____						Self
						Teacher
Date ____ / ____ / _____						Self
						Teacher
Date ____ / ____ / _____						Self
						Teacher
Total Points						

Scoring Guide

Did you **complete the Daily Do Now?**	+1
Did you use the **correct word form?**	+1
Did you add **relevant content?**	+2
Did you add content using **correct grammar?**	+1

	Complete Do Now	Correct Word Form	Relevant Content	Correct Grammar	Total	
Date ____ / ____ / _____						Self
						Teacher
Date ____ / ____ / _____						Self
						Teacher
Date ____ / ____ / _____						Self
						Teacher
Date ____ / ____ / _____						Self
						Teacher
Date ____ / ____ / _____						Self
						Teacher
Total Points						

Daily Do Now

Record the Daily Do Now at the beginning of each
class. Complete the task using the correct word form,
relevant content, and correct grammar.

	Scores					
	Complete Do Now	Correct Word Form	Relevant Content	Correct Grammar	Total	
Date ____ / ____ / _____						Self
						Teacher
Date ____ / ____ / _____						Self
						Teacher
Date ____ / ____ / _____						Self
						Teacher
Date ____ / ____ / _____						Self
						Teacher
Date ____ / ____ / _____						Self
						Teacher
Total Points						

Scoring Guide

Did you **complete the Daily Do Now?**	+1
Did you use the **correct word form**?	+1
Did you add **relevant content**?	+2
Did you add content using **correct grammar**?	+1

	Scores				
	Complete Do Now	Correct Word Form	Relevant Content	Correct Grammar	Total

Date _____ / _____ / _____

Self

Teacher

Date _____ / _____ / _____

Self

Teacher

Date _____ / _____ / _____

Self

Teacher

Date _____ / _____ / _____

Self

Teacher

Date _____ / _____ / _____

Self

Teacher

Total Points

Daily Do Now

Record the Daily Do Now at the beginning of each class. Complete the task using the correct word form, relevant content, and correct grammar.

	Scores					
	Complete Do Now	Correct Word Form	Relevant Content	Correct Grammar	Total	

Date _____ / _____ / _____

— Self

— Teacher

Date _____ / _____ / _____

— Self

— Teacher

Date _____ / _____ / _____

— Self

— Teacher

Date _____ / _____ / _____

— Self

— Teacher

Date _____ / _____ / _____

— Self

— Teacher

Total Points

Scoring Guide

Did you **complete the Daily Do Now**?	+1
Did you use the **correct word form**?	+1
Did you add **relevant content**?	+2
Did you add content using **correct grammar**?	+1

Scores					
Complete Do Now	Correct Word Form	Relevant Content	Correct Grammar	Total	

Date _____ / _____ / _____

| | | | | | Self |
| | | | | | Teacher |

Date _____ / _____ / _____

| | | | | | Self |
| | | | | | Teacher |

Date _____ / _____ / _____

| | | | | | Self |
| | | | | | Teacher |

Date _____ / _____ / _____

| | | | | | Self |
| | | | | | Teacher |

Date _____ / _____ / _____

| | | | | | Self |
| | | | | | Teacher |

Total Points

Daily Do Now

Record the Daily Do Now at the beginning of each class. Complete the task using the correct word form, relevant content, and correct grammar.

	Complete Do Now	Correct Word Form	Relevant Content	Correct Grammar	Total	
Scores						
Date ____ / ____ / _____						Self
						Teacher
Date ____ / ____ / _____						Self
						Teacher
Date ____ / ____ / _____						Self
						Teacher
Date ____ / ____ / _____						Self
						Teacher
Date ____ / ____ / _____						Self
						Teacher
Total Points						

Scoring Guide

Did you **complete the Daily Do Now**?	+1
Did you use the **correct word form**?	+1
Did you add **relevant content**?	+2
Did you add content using **correct grammar**?	+1

Scores					
Complete Do Now	Correct Word Form	Relevant Content	Correct Grammar	Total	

Date _____ / _____ / _____

| | | | | | Self |
| | | | | | Teacher |

Date _____ / _____ / _____

| | | | | | Self |
| | | | | | Teacher |

Date _____ / _____ / _____

| | | | | | Self |
| | | | | | Teacher |

Date _____ / _____ / _____

| | | | | | Self |
| | | | | | Teacher |

Date _____ / _____ / _____

| | | | | | Self |
| | | | | | Teacher |

Total Points

Daily Do Now

Record the Daily Do Now at the beginning of each class. Complete the task using the correct word form, relevant content, and correct grammar.

	Scores					
	Complete Do Now	Correct Word Form	Relevant Content	Correct Grammar	Total	

Date _____ / _____ / _____						Self
						Teacher
Date _____ / _____ / _____						Self
						Teacher
Date _____ / _____ / _____						Self
						Teacher
Date _____ / _____ / _____						Self
						Teacher
Date _____ / _____ / _____						Self
						Teacher

Total Points

Scoring Guide

Did you **complete the Daily Do Now**?	+1
Did you use the **correct word form**?	+1
Did you add **relevant content**?	+2
Did you add content using **correct grammar**?	+1

Scores					
Complete Do Now	Correct Word Form	Relevant Content	Correct Grammar	Total	

Date _____ / _____ / _____

					Self
					Teacher

Date _____ / _____ / _____

					Self
					Teacher

Date _____ / _____ / _____

					Self
					Teacher

Date _____ / _____ / _____

					Self
					Teacher

Date _____ / _____ / _____

					Self
					Teacher

Total Points

Daily Do Now

Record the Daily Do Now at the beginning of each class. Complete the task using the correct word form, relevant content, and correct grammar.

	Scores					
	Complete Do Now	Correct Word Form	Relevant Content	Correct Grammar	Total	

Date _____ / _____ / _____

_____

_____

_____

| Self |
| Teacher |

Date _____ / _____ / _____

_____

_____

_____

| Self |
| Teacher |

Date _____ / _____ / _____

_____

_____

_____

| Self |
| Teacher |

Date _____ / _____ / _____

_____

_____

_____

| Self |
| Teacher |

Date _____ / _____ / _____

_____

_____

_____

| Self |
| Teacher |

Total Points

Scoring Guide

Did you **complete the Daily Do Now**?	+1
Did you use the **correct word form**?	+1
Did you add **relevant content**?	+2
Did you add content using **correct grammar**?	+1

	Complete Do Now	Correct Word Form	Relevant Content	Correct Grammar	Total	
						Scores

Date _____ / _____ / _____

| | | | | | | Self |
| | | | | | | Teacher |

Date _____ / _____ / _____

| | | | | | | Self |
| | | | | | | Teacher |

Date _____ / _____ / _____

| | | | | | | Self |
| | | | | | | Teacher |

Date _____ / _____ / _____

| | | | | | | Self |
| | | | | | | Teacher |

Date _____ / _____ / _____

| | | | | | | Self |
| | | | | | | Teacher |

Total Points

Daily Do Now

Record the Daily Do Now at the beginning of each class. Complete the task using the correct word form, relevant content, and correct grammar.

	Scores				
	Complete Do Now	Correct Word Form	Relevant Content	Correct Grammar	Total

Date _____ / _____ / _____
_____
_____
_____
_____

Self

Teacher

Date _____ / _____ / _____
_____
_____
_____
_____

Self

Teacher

Date _____ / _____ / _____
_____
_____
_____
_____

Self

Teacher

Date _____ / _____ / _____
_____
_____
_____
_____

Self

Teacher

Date _____ / _____ / _____
_____
_____
_____
_____

Self

Teacher

Total Points

Scoring Guide

Did you **complete the Daily Do Now**?	+1
Did you use the **correct word form**?	+1
Did you add **relevant content**?	+2
Did you add content using **correct grammar**?	+1

	Scores					
	Complete Do Now	Correct Word Form	Relevant Content	Correct Grammar	Total	

Date _____ / _____ / _____

| | | | | | Self |
| | | | | | Teacher |

Date _____ / _____ / _____

| | | | | | Self |
| | | | | | Teacher |

Date _____ / _____ / _____

| | | | | | Self |
| | | | | | Teacher |

Date _____ / _____ / _____

| | | | | | Self |
| | | | | | Teacher |

Date _____ / _____ / _____

| | | | | | Self |
| | | | | | Teacher |

Total Points

Daily Do Now

Record the Daily Do Now at the beginning of each class. Complete the task using the correct word form, relevant content, and correct grammar.

	Scores					
	Complete Do Now	Correct Word Form	Relevant Content	Correct Grammar	Total	

Date _____ / _____ / _____

_____

_____

_____

_____ — Self

_____ — Teacher

Date _____ / _____ / _____

_____

_____

_____

_____ — Self

_____ — Teacher

Date _____ / _____ / _____

_____

_____

_____

_____ — Self

_____ — Teacher

Date _____ / _____ / _____

_____

_____

_____

_____ — Self

_____ — Teacher

Date _____ / _____ / _____

_____

_____

_____

_____ — Self

_____ — Teacher

Total Points

Scoring Guide

Did you **complete the Daily Do Now**?	+1
Did you use the **correct word form**?	+1
Did you add **relevant content**?	+2
Did you add content using **correct grammar**?	+1

	Scores					
	Complete Do Now	Correct Word Form	Relevant Content	Correct Grammar	Total	

Date _____ / _____ / _____

| | | | | | | Self |
| | | | | | | Teacher |

Date _____ / _____ / _____

| | | | | | | Self |
| | | | | | | Teacher |

Date _____ / _____ / _____

| | | | | | | Self |
| | | | | | | Teacher |

Date _____ / _____ / _____

| | | | | | | Self |
| | | | | | | Teacher |

Date _____ / _____ / _____

| | | | | | | Self |
| | | | | | | Teacher |

Total Points

Daily Do Now

Record the Daily Do Now at the beginning of each class. Complete the task using the correct word form, relevant content, and correct grammar.

	Scores					
	Complete Do Now	Correct Word Form	Relevant Content	Correct Grammar	Total	

Date _____ / _____ / _____

_____

_____

_____

_____

| | | | | | Self |
| | | | | | Teacher |

Date _____ / _____ / _____

_____

_____

_____

_____

| | | | | | Self |
| | | | | | Teacher |

Date _____ / _____ / _____

_____

_____

_____

_____

| | | | | | Self |
| | | | | | Teacher |

Date _____ / _____ / _____

_____

_____

_____

_____

| | | | | | Self |
| | | | | | Teacher |

Date _____ / _____ / _____

_____

_____

_____

_____

| | | | | | Self |
| | | | | | Teacher |

Total Points

Scoring Guide

Did you **complete the Daily Do Now**?	+1
Did you use the **correct word form**?	+1
Did you add **relevant content**?	+2
Did you add content using **correct grammar**?	+1

	Complete Do Now	Correct Word Form	Relevant Content	Correct Grammar	Total	
Scores						
Date ____ / ____ / _____						Self
						Teacher
Date ____ / ____ / _____						Self
						Teacher
Date ____ / ____ / _____						Self
						Teacher
Date ____ / ____ / _____						Self
						Teacher
Date ____ / ____ / _____						Self
						Teacher
Total Points						

Daily Do Now

Record the Daily Do Now at the beginning of each class. Complete the task using the correct word form, relevant content, and correct grammar.

	Scores					
	Complete Do Now	Correct Word Form	Relevant Content	Correct Grammar	Total	
Date ____ / ____ / _____						Self
						Teacher
Date ____ / ____ / _____						Self
						Teacher
Date ____ / ____ / _____						Self
						Teacher
Date ____ / ____ / _____						Self
						Teacher
Date ____ / ____ / _____						Self
						Teacher
Total Points						

Scoring Guide

Did you **complete the Daily Do Now**?	**+1**
Did you use the **correct word form**?	**+1**
Did you add **relevant content**?	**+2**
Did you add content using **correct grammar**?	**+1**

Scores					
Complete Do Now	Correct Word Form	Relevant Content	Correct Grammar	Total	

Date _____ / _____ / _____

					Self
					Teacher

Date _____ / _____ / _____

					Self
					Teacher

Date _____ / _____ / _____

					Self
					Teacher

Date _____ / _____ / _____

					Self
					Teacher

Date _____ / _____ / _____

					Self
					Teacher

Total Points

Daily Do Now

Record the Daily Do Now at the beginning of each class. Complete the task using the correct word form, relevant content, and correct grammar.

	Scores					
	Complete Do Now	Correct Word Form	Relevant Content	Correct Grammar	Total	

Date _____ / _____ / _____

						Self
						Teacher

Date _____ / _____ / _____

						Self
						Teacher

Date _____ / _____ / _____

						Self
						Teacher

Date _____ / _____ / _____

						Self
						Teacher

Date _____ / _____ / _____

						Self
						Teacher

Total Points

Scoring Guide

Did you **complete the Daily Do Now**?	+1
Did you use the **correct word form**?	+1
Did you add **relevant content**?	+2
Did you add content using **correct grammar**?	+1

	Scores					
	Complete Do Now	Correct Word Form	Relevant Content	Correct Grammar	Total	
Date ____ / ____ / ____						Self
						Teacher
Date ____ / ____ / ____						Self
						Teacher
Date ____ / ____ / ____						Self
						Teacher
Date ____ / ____ / ____						Self
						Teacher
Date ____ / ____ / ____						Self
						Teacher
Total Points						

Daily Do Now

Record the Daily Do Now at the beginning of each class. Complete the task using the correct word form, relevant content, and correct grammar.

	Scores					
	Complete Do Now	Correct Word Form	Relevant Content	Correct Grammar	Total	

Date _____ / _____ / _____

| | | | | | | Self |
| | | | | | | Teacher |

Date _____ / _____ / _____

| | | | | | | Self |
| | | | | | | Teacher |

Date _____ / _____ / _____

| | | | | | | Self |
| | | | | | | Teacher |

Date _____ / _____ / _____

| | | | | | | Self |
| | | | | | | Teacher |

Date _____ / _____ / _____

| | | | | | | Self |
| | | | | | | Teacher |

Total Points

Scoring Guide

Did you **complete the Daily Do Now**?	+1
Did you use the **correct word form**?	+1
Did you add **relevant content**?	+2
Did you add content using **correct grammar**?	+1

Scores

Complete Do Now	Correct Word Form	Relevant Content	Correct Grammar	Total	

Date _____ / _____ / _____

| | | | | | Self |
| | | | | | Teacher |

Date _____ / _____ / _____

| | | | | | Self |
| | | | | | Teacher |

Date _____ / _____ / _____

| | | | | | Self |
| | | | | | Teacher |

Date _____ / _____ / _____

| | | | | | Self |
| | | | | | Teacher |

Date _____ / _____ / _____

| | | | | | Self |
| | | | | | Teacher |

Total Points

Daily Do Now

Record the Daily Do Now at the beginning of each class. Complete the task using the correct word form, relevant content, and correct grammar.

	Scores				
	Complete Do Now	Correct Word Form	Relevant Content	Correct Grammar	Total

Date _____ / _____ / _____

_____

_____

_____

_____

Self

Teacher

Date _____ / _____ / _____

_____

_____

_____

_____

Self

Teacher

Date _____ / _____ / _____

_____

_____

_____

_____

Self

Teacher

Date _____ / _____ / _____

_____

_____

_____

_____

Self

Teacher

Date _____ / _____ / _____

_____

_____

_____

_____

Self

Teacher

Total Points

Scoring Guide

Did you **complete the Daily Do Now**?	+1
Did you use the **correct word form**?	+1
Did you add **relevant content**?	+2
Did you add content using **correct grammar**?	+1

	Scores				
Complete Do Now	Correct Word Form	Relevant Content	Correct Grammar	Total	

Date _____ / _____ / _____

					Self
					Teacher

Date _____ / _____ / _____

					Self
					Teacher

Date _____ / _____ / _____

					Self
					Teacher

Date _____ / _____ / _____

					Self
					Teacher

Date _____ / _____ / _____

					Self
					Teacher

Total Points

Daily Do Now

Record the Daily Do Now at the beginning of each class. Complete the task using the correct word form, relevant vocabulary, and correct grammar.

	Scores					
	Complete Do Now	Correct Word Form	Relevant Content	Correct Grammar	Total	

Date _____ / _____ / _____

_____

_____

_____

_____

					Self
					Teacher

Date _____ / _____ / _____

_____

_____

_____

_____

					Self
					Teacher

Date _____ / _____ / _____

_____

_____

_____

_____

					Self
					Teacher

Date _____ / _____ / _____

_____

_____

_____

_____

					Self
					Teacher

Date _____ / _____ / _____

_____

_____

_____

_____

					Self
					Teacher

Total Points

Scoring Guide

Did you **complete the Daily Do Now**?	+1
Did you use the **correct word form**?	+1
Did you add **relevant content**?	+2
Did you add content using **correct grammar**?	+1

	Scores					
	Complete Do Now	Correct Word Form	Relevant Content	Correct Grammar	Total	

Date _____ / _____ / _____

					Self
					Teacher

Date _____ / _____ / _____

					Self
					Teacher

Date _____ / _____ / _____

					Self
					Teacher

Date _____ / _____ / _____

					Self
					Teacher

Date _____ / _____ / _____

					Self
					Teacher

Total Points

Daily Do Now

Record the Daily Do Now at the beginning of each class. Complete the task using the correct word form, relevant vocabulary, and correct grammar.

	Scores					
	Complete Do Now	Correct Word Form	Relevant Content	Correct Grammar	Total	

Date _____ / _____ / _____

| | | | | | Self |
| | | | | | Teacher |

Date _____ / _____ / _____

| | | | | | Self |
| | | | | | Teacher |

Date _____ / _____ / _____

| | | | | | Self |
| | | | | | Teacher |

Date _____ / _____ / _____

| | | | | | Self |
| | | | | | Teacher |

Date _____ / _____ / _____

| | | | | | Self |
| | | | | | Teacher |

Total Points

Scoring Guide

Did you **complete the Daily Do Now**?	+1
Did you use the **correct word form**?	+1
Did you add **relevant content**?	+2
Did you add content using **correct grammar**?	+1

	Scores					
	Complete Do Now	Correct Word Form	Relevant Content	Correct Grammar	Total	

Date _____ / _____ / _____

| | | | | | Self |
| | | | | | Teacher |

Date _____ / _____ / _____

| | | | | | Self |
| | | | | | Teacher |

Date _____ / _____ / _____

| | | | | | Self |
| | | | | | Teacher |

Date _____ / _____ / _____

| | | | | | Self |
| | | | | | Teacher |

Date _____ / _____ / _____

| | | | | | Self |
| | | | | | Teacher |

Total Points

Daily Do Now

Record the Daily Do Now at the beginning of each class. Complete the task using the correct word form, relevant vocabulary, and correct grammar.

	Scores					
	Complete Do Now	Correct Word Form	Relevant Content	Correct Grammar	Total	

Date _____ / _____ / _____						Self
						Teacher
Date _____ / _____ / _____						Self
						Teacher
Date _____ / _____ / _____						Self
						Teacher
Date _____ / _____ / _____						Self
						Teacher
Date _____ / _____ / _____						Self
						Teacher

Total Points

Scoring Guide

Did you **complete the Daily Do Now**?	**+1**
Did you use the **correct word form**?	**+1**
Did you add **relevant content**?	**+2**
Did you add content using **correct grammar**?	**+1**

	Scores					
	Complete Do Now	Correct Word Form	Relevant Content	Correct Grammar	Total	

Date _____ / _____ / _____

| | | | | | | Self |
| | | | | | | Teacher |

Date _____ / _____ / _____

| | | | | | | Self |
| | | | | | | Teacher |

Date _____ / _____ / _____

| | | | | | | Self |
| | | | | | | Teacher |

Date _____ / _____ / _____

| | | | | | | Self |
| | | | | | | Teacher |

Date _____ / _____ / _____

| | | | | | | Self |
| | | | | | | Teacher |

Total Points

Daily Do Now

Record the Daily Do Now at the beginning of each class. Complete the task using the correct word form, relevant content, and correct grammar.

	Scores					
	Complete Do Now	Correct Word Form	Relevant Content	Correct Grammar	Total	
Date ___ / ___ / _____						Self
						Teacher
Date ___ / ___ / _____						Self
						Teacher
Date ___ / ___ / _____						Self
						Teacher
Date ___ / ___ / _____						Self
						Teacher
Date ___ / ___ / _____						Self
						Teacher
Total Points						

Scoring Guide

Did you **complete the Daily Do Now**?	+1
Did you use the **correct word form**?	+1
Did you add **relevant content**?	+2
Did you add content using **correct grammar**?	+1

	Scores					
	Complete Do Now	Correct Word Form	Relevant Content	Correct Grammar	Total	

Date _____ / _____ / _____

| | | | | | Self |
| | | | | | Teacher |

Date _____ / _____ / _____

| | | | | | Self |
| | | | | | Teacher |

Date _____ / _____ / _____

| | | | | | Self |
| | | | | | Teacher |

Date _____ / _____ / _____

| | | | | | Self |
| | | | | | Teacher |

Date _____ / _____ / _____

| | | | | | Self |
| | | | | | Teacher |

Total Points

Daily Do Now

Record the Daily Do Now at the beginning of each class. Complete the task using the correct word form, relevant content, and correct grammar.

	Scores					
	Complete Do Now	Correct Word Form	Relevant Content	Correct Grammar	Total	
Date ____ / ____ / _____						Self
						Teacher
Date ____ / ____ / _____						Self
						Teacher
Date ____ / ____ / _____						Self
						Teacher
Date ____ / ____ / _____						Self
						Teacher
Date ____ / ____ / _____						Self
						Teacher
Total Points						

Scoring Guide

Did you **complete the Daily Do Now**?	+1
Did you use the **correct word form**?	+1
Did you add **relevant content**?	+2
Did you add content using **correct grammar**?	+1

	Scores					
	Complete Do Now	Correct Word Form	Relevant Content	Correct Grammar	Total	

Date _____ / _____ / _____

						Self
						Teacher

Date _____ / _____ / _____

						Self
						Teacher

Date _____ / _____ / _____

						Self
						Teacher

Date _____ / _____ / _____

						Self
						Teacher

Date _____ / _____ / _____

						Self
						Teacher

Total Points

Daily Do Now

Record the Daily Do Now at the beginning of each class. Complete the task using the correct word form, relevant content, and correct grammar.

	Scores					
	Complete Do Now	Correct Word Form	Relevant Content	Correct Grammar	Total	

Date _____ / _____ / _____

_____

_____

_____

_____

Self

Teacher

Date _____ / _____ / _____

_____

_____

_____

_____

Self

Teacher

Date _____ / _____ / _____

_____

_____

_____

_____

Self

Teacher

Date _____ / _____ / _____

_____

_____

_____

_____

Self

Teacher

Date _____ / _____ / _____

_____

_____

_____

_____

Self

Teacher

Total Points

Scoring Guide

Did you **complete the Daily Do Now**?	+1
Did you use the **correct word form**?	+1
Did you add **relevant content**?	+2
Did you add content using **correct grammar**?	+1

	Scores					
	Complete Do Now	Correct Word Form	Relevant Content	Correct Grammar	Total	

| Date ____ / ____ / ____ | | | | | | Self |
| | | | | | | Teacher |

| Date ____ / ____ / ____ | | | | | | Self |
| | | | | | | Teacher |

| Date ____ / ____ / ____ | | | | | | Self |
| | | | | | | Teache˞ |

| Date ____ / ____ / ____ | | | | | | Self |
| | | | | | | Teacher |

| Date ____ / ____ / ____ | | | | | | Self |
| | | | | | | Teacher |

Total Points